# CYCLING
# RIGHTS

ISBN: 978-1-63385-395-9

*Designed and published by*
Word Association Publishers
205 Fifth Avenue
Tarentum, Pennsylvania 15084

www.wordassociation.com
1.800.827.7903

# CYCLING RIGHTS

## BICYCLES, E-BIKES & MICRO-MOBILITY DEVICES

### KENNETH J. KNABE
**GREATER CLEVELAND'S BIKE ATTORNEY**
WITH PARKER MULHOLLAND

WORD ASSOCIATION PUBLISHERS
www.wordassociation.com
1.800.827.7903

# FOREWARD

## BY
## MARK
## J. LOONEY

# KNABE LAW FIRM, IN THE "HUB" OF IT ALL . . .

**G**reater Cleveland's bike scene is continually expanding into a premier destination for cyclists. Once the nation's fifth largest city, Cleveland's formerly gritty steampunk roads are transforming, offering a wonderful dichotomy of bike travels via city street painted lanes, towpath gravel grinders, protected bike lanes, and bike trails for commuters, enthusiasts, and aspiring competitors. To reach out beyond your backyard, the Cleveland area will entertain the senses with lake views, historic canals, numerous parks including a National Park right on our doorstep, and diverse city cultures . . . each conveniently connected by an ever growing network of bike paths.

During my early Cleveland bike travels I became associated with a bike shop called "Spin" located on Madison Avenue just down the street from Ken Knabe's law firm in Lakewood. Central to the Wednesday rides were the personalities. Ken quickly made his presence known, ensuring lights were on and blinking at sundown. He taught us disciplined awareness of our surroundings and adherence to the laws of the road. Our knowledge of the law came from the confidence communicated by fellow cyclist Ken Knabe. With this book, Ken adds "author" to his own list of accomplishments. The information he shares is of equal value to the beginner, intermediate or advanced cyclist as well as other road users.

Cyclists take many forms in the Cleveland area, each requiring specific equipment and road space to exercise their craft. In 2018, Ken and two other cyclists joined me for a four-day ride on the Ohio to Erie Trail ("OTET" for short). A 326-mile-long endeavor, we traveled from Cleveland to Millersburg; Millersburg to Columbus; Columbus to Yellow Springs; and Yellow Springs to Cincinnati along wonderful park-like settings and bike trails. It was an adventure many are beginning to discover, starting from the shores of Lake Erie at Edgewater Park. With Ken's emphasis on safety and injury prevention while riding, we completed our mission all in one piece, with zero injuries or close calls!

Cyclists can face tough issues, situations and decisions, and Ken's book takes on and answers many pressing questions related to cycling. I travel the country by bicycle greatly comforted by the knowledge that I have friends like Ken working to make our byways safe for road users of all types. I carry Ken's phone number in my jersey in the unlikely event of injury while enjoying the roads less traveled. If you run into Ken at an upcoming cycling event, be sure to reach out and introduce yourself. You may hear about some of the other new and exciting projects he is working on.

*Mark J. Looney,*

Member of the Board of Directors for the Ohio to Erie Trail (OTET)

Author of *A Path Through Ohio, A Cyclist's Guide to The Ohio to Erie Trail (Third Edition)* and the forthcoming *Lake Effect: A Cyclist's Guide Around the Great Lakes*

Trans-Am Soloist 1983

# AUTHOR'S PREFACE

## BY
## KENNETH
## J. KNABE

I n March 2020, Gov. Mike DeWine declared that bicycle shops are **essential** businesses in Ohio. Why?

Because many people use bikes for transportation, and the health benefits of riding are legion. Rapid changes in our cycling environment occur and familiarity with the associated laws and the safety aspects is essential in our new world. I address issues that are important to cyclists and motorists so we can have safer roads. Due to the uptick in new cyclists since the onset of the global pandemic, I've seen many new cyclists out on the streets without lights on at sundown and riding against traffic! All riders should know the laws that are designed to protect them. Please read whatever chapter speaks to you, and certainly consider reading them all as they are founts of valuable information for all riders.

With years of cycling experience combined with my background as a trial lawyer, guiding fellow cyclists is a calling to me. Why should you, as a cyclist, a rider and/or motorist, read this book?

**The reason is twofold.**

**First**, to help you understand your rights and responsibilities as we strive toward calmer, safer roads where bikes, micromobility devices, pedestrians, and motor vehicles truly "share the road" as co-equal users. As an avid cyclist these issues affect my everyday life. Safe bike infrastructure is growing exponentially thanks to organizations like Bike Cleveland and the Ohio Bicycle Federation (OBF); agencies such as the Northeast Ohio Areawide Coordinating Agency (NOACA) and the Cleveland Metroparks; numerous bike clubs; specific efforts such as the Ohio to Erie Trail (OTET); and other initiatives like the City of Cleveland's upcoming Vision Zero legislation. We must continue adapting our knowledge along with these advancements and ensure no road user is left behind.

**Second**, when a fellow cyclist is hit and injured by an unsafe motorist, the cyclist needs to know the appropriate steps to take to protect themselves.

Bike Law is now the primary focus of my personal injury law practice. Why?

**For personal reasons.**

I've also been knocked off my bike and injured by a verbally aggressive hit-and-run motorist. I know how it felt to be left on the pavement, half clipped in with absolutely no concern on the motorist's part as to whether I was okay. I have many clients who've been hit and seriously injured, and I've lost a friend to a fatal bike crash. While cycling is generally safe in Ohio, I provide for reference an outline of what a cyclist and their family should do to obtain the justice they deserve in the unfortunate event of a crash. I also provide numerous tips on avoiding crashes because as the saying goes, an ounce of prevention can be worth a pound of cure.

I hope this book is helpful as you navigate our complex world from the saddle of your bike, the platform of your e-scooter, or behind the wheel of your motor vehicle.

With many thanks for their invaluable contributions to: Lisa Parker Green of Parker Mulholland LLC[I] for editing and writing expertise; Keith Berr and Linda Barberic of Keith Berr Productions[II] for photographic direction and excellence; Jacob VanSickle, Executive Director of Bike Cleveland;[III] Cleveland Councilman Matt Zone;[IV] Cleveland cyclist and Vision Zero advocate Ashley Shaw;[V] author Mark J. Looney (*A Path Through*

*Ohio)*;[VI] attorney Sean Allan for guidance regarding insurance law; paralegal Lisa Duchnowski for her valuable ideas and input; Patricia Kovacs and Chuck Smith of Ohio Bicycle Federation (OBF)[VII] and their colleague Sharon Montgomery; Calley Mersmann, as of this writing Cleveland's Bicycle and Pedestrian Coordinator; and Anne Tillie of Cleveland City Council for dedicated cycling advocacy and generous sharing of information; Knabe Law Firm Office Manager Michele Hohm for her support throughout the creation of this book; Matt McLaughlin of Lakewood for exceptional illustrations; and the very knowledgeable and insightful, future lawyer and Cat. 1 cyclist Rob Thompson.

*Kenneth J. Knabe*
Lakewood, Ohio
July 17, 2020

*All profits from the sale of this book will be donated to Bike Cleveland and other local and state bike organizations, shops and clubs.*

*As it becomes available, information and updates regarding legislation, cycling laws, and more can be found at:*

https://klfohio.com/cycling-rights-book/

I.   https://www.parkermulhollandllc.com/

II.  https://www.keithberr.com/

III. https://www.bikecleveland.org/about/staff-board/

IV.  https://clevelandcitycouncil.org/ward-15

V.   http://www.ohiocity.org/staff

VI.  https://www.amazon.com/dp/0998220434/

VII. http://www.ohiobike.org/

# TABLE OF CONTENTS

# 1

# LEGAL BIKE PRACTICE

n this initial chapter I share a little more about myself as both a cyclist and an attorney. If you'd prefer to get right to the nitty-gritty regarding your rights and responsibilities, feel free to skip ahead to the next chapter.

I've been riding bikes since I was a kid and cycling is a major part of my life. I enjoy both the physical and psychological benefits, and the challenge and camaraderie, offered by the open road. I've ridden many century rides, have cycled toward a cure for cancer with Velosano,[1] and have traversed the 326-mile Ohio to Erie Trail (OTET)[2] and the Great Allegheny Passage (The GAP). I'm on my road bike several times a week in decent weather, and in the winter I ride indoors on my trainer.[3] I have a three-bike quiver: a road bike, a gravel bike, and my trusty commuter.

I protect and support fellow Ohio cyclists in numerous ways beyond representing them when they are injured in a crash. The Cleveland City Council Safety Committee's **Vision Zero Taskforce**—detailed in the Spring 2018 edition of Councilman (and Safety Committee Chairman) Matt Zone's *In the Zone*[4]— has appointed me Co-Chair of the Maintenance and Vehicle Fleet Subcommittee, along with my colleague and friend Terrell Cole, Deputy Chief Operating Officer, Cleveland. The goal of Vision Zero safety strategy legislation is "to eliminate all traffic fatalities and serious injuries on our roads and increase safety and equitable mobility for **all** road users—bikes, motor vehicles and pedestrians alike".[5]

I was honored at the Bike Cleveland[6] 2019 Annual Meeting to receive the **Guardian of Sustainable Transportation Award** for supporting local advocacy including Bike Cleveland and sponsoring their annual "Fundo," Bike to Work and Bike to School events, Vision Zero legislation, and representing Greater Cleveland cyclists injured by unsafe motorists.

I'm a Board Member of the Ohio Bicycle Federation (OBF)[7] and the Ohio to Erie Trail (OTET), a sponsor of VeloFemme-Litzer[8]—a female race and development team, and Team Spin/Litzler Automation[9]—a male racing team, a "Kilo Sponsor" of

The Guardian of Sustainable Transportation Award Bike Cleveland: Executive Director Jacob VanSickle (left), Ken Knabe (center), Communications & Events Manager Jason Kuhn (right)

Cleveland Velodrome[10]—a dedicated bike racing complex in Cleveland, and I'm a League of American Bicyclists[11] Advocate Member.

Publishing and lecturing on bike safety factors heavily in my advocacy for the cycling community, including authoring bike law articles and co-authoring the *Bikes and the Law* section on Bike Cleveland's website[12] as well as teaching Continuing Legal Education (C.L.E.) to Ohio attorneys on how to properly handle a bike crash case. I've written safety advisories for many bike events and have presented in front of local bike clubs and organizations, passing along important safety and legal information to riders in an effort to promote awareness.

I've been a trial attorney for 30 years specializing in representing the injured. I'm also an avid cyclist. The combination makes me a true bike lawyer. In short, I am always protecting cyclists!

# 2

# KNOWLEDGE IS POWER

## CYCLIST RIGHTS & RESPONSIBILITIES

**A**s far back as 1597, Sir Francis Bacon knew that "*Ipsa scientia potestas est*" ("Knowledge itself is power").[13] Hundreds of years later this adage couldn't be more accurate!

# CYCLIST RIGHTS & RESPONSIBILITIES ACCORDING TO OHIO LAW

Familiarity with Ohio's bike laws is imperative for legal bike riding. Cyclists—and motorists—should be aware of the numerous and evolving laws on the books. Look first to Ohio traffic laws contained in the Ohio Revised Code (ORC) under Title 45. Local authorities regulate bike operation independently to a degree, but no local ordinance can be fundamentally inconsistent with the ORC.[14] The Ohio Department of Transportation (ODOT) also has a very helpful booklet containing Ohio bike laws **and** cycling tips that promote safety for all road users.[15]

## A BIKE IS A VEHICLE

**A bicycle is a legal road vehicle in Ohio.**[16 & 17] As such, most traffic laws that pertain to a "vehicle" apply to bicycles.[18] Bikes don't **block** traffic, they **are** traffic. Cyclists are not **in** motorists' way, they are **on** their **own** way!

Cyclists may be familiar with the term "vehicular cycling" and some of the debate surrounding it. Originally coined by advocate and author, the late John Forester[19] in his 1976 book *Effective Cycling,*[20] the term "vehicular cycling" means (to this author) **riding our bikes on the road similarly to the way we drive our motor vehicles,** following the applicable traffic laws. John Forester and the vehicular cycling contingent deserve credit for their important work in helping to define bicycles as vehicles with road rights. But this author also believes in dedicated bike infrastructure like bike lanes including protected bike lanes, bike boxes, bicycle specific signals, and other bike specific road safety measures.

# CYCLISTS HAVE A LEGAL RIGHT TO RIDE ON THE ROAD

In Ohio, adult cyclists have an **absolute legal right to ride on the road** except on divided, controlled access freeways.[21 & 22 & 23] The selective exclusion signage for certain vehicles and situations is published in the Ohio Manual of Uniform Traffic Control Devices under their "R5" series signage. The most common signs restricting bikes are the R5-10a, R5-10b, and the R5-6 sign pictured here.

Cycling on the road is legal—except on divided, controlled access freeways

# CYCLISTS ALSO PAY FOR ROADS

Many motorists assert they should have priority on our roads because they "pay" for them through registration, gas tax, and licensing fees, and therefore "own" the road. This, however, is a misconception. While it is true that motorists pay tolls, gas tax, and registration fees (collectively "user fees"), they only make up 55% of Ohio's road budget.[24] The rest is comprised of general funds that come primarily from property tax and sales tax paid by people whether they drive a motor vehicle or not. If motorists were to bear the full brunt of the cost of our roads, the gas tax would need to be raised by over 75% to $0.50/gallon. In 2019—during which there was a 28-cent tax per gallon of gas—Ohio lawmakers began contemplating raising the gas tax to provide at least part of the $1 billion needed for all road and bridge repair.[25] To add insult to injury, people generally ride on local streets, and these roads are paid for primarily with local property taxes and other sources of general revenue. Moreover, the reason roads are so expensive is that they are costly to maintain due to motor vehicles damaging them in a way that bicycles simply do not. To wit, a two-hundred-pound bicyclist with a fifty-pound bike will impose approximately **1/65,000th** the roadway damage of a four-thousand-pound motor vehicle![26] And once you start factoring in external costs of driving such as air and water pollution, it ends up costing society twenty-nine-cents a mile to drive a motor vehicle, while a person on a bike generates an external cost of less than a penny a mile.

Ultimately, the misconception is not only wrong, but reversed! People who bike, instead of driving, pay a much bigger share through their general fund contributions than motorists do through their user fee contributions; plus, a heavy majority of cyclists also own and drive motor vehicles so they pay those fees, too, but on balance create far less damage and subsequent cost.[27] Cyclists not only belong on the roads, they cover their costs, something motorists have never been asked to do. And yet, as discussed in Carlton Reid's *Roads Were Not Built for Cars*,[28] our modern roadways were initially paved due to a bicycle boom in the early 1900s before motor vehicles were even available.

# CYCLISTS CAN'T BE CONFINED TO SIDEWALKS OR ALL PURPOSE TRAILS

**Ohio law provides that cyclists cannot be restricted to riding on a sidewalk,** and many local ordinances even make it illegal to ride on a sidewalk in a business district. Sidewalks are frequently pockmarked, uneven, too close for a backing motor vehicle driver to see a cyclist, and littered, often containing gravel, dangerous sewers, glass, and debris. More than the physical condition of the sidewalks, cyclists can constitute a real hazard to pedestrians including slower walkers and parents pushing baby strollers. For cyclists, sidewalks may not always be a safe alternative to roadways.

Beyond traditional sidewalks, **cyclists also can't be confined to riding on the all purpose trails in the Metroparks or elsewhere.**[29 & 30] So, please keep in mind that the people you see riding their bikes on the road in the Cleveland Metroparks (for example) are doing so legally. Remember—it's a park, not a freeway; and you bought a motor vehicle, you didn't buy the whole road!

Cyclists have a legal right to ride on the road including in the Metroparks

# WHERE DO WE RIDE ON THE ROAD?

Ohio law provides that we must ride as near to the right side of the roadway as is "**practicable**" i.e., basically reasonable.[31] If it's unsafe for a cyclist to ride at the far right side of a roadway, it's not required. Valid reasons exist for not staying at the road's right side including avoiding fixed or moving objects—such as parked or moving vehicles—and hazardous surfaces. If the lane is too narrow for a motor vehicle to safely pass a cyclist, the cyclist can take the full (whole) lane, and the motorist **must** wait for an opportunity to safely pass the cyclist (or group of cyclists).[32] A motorist is legally allowed to safely cross a double yellow line to pass slower bikes subject to these precautions:

- The cyclist is traveling at less than half the posted speed limit

- The motorist shall not exceed the speed limit while making the pass, and

- There is sufficient clear sight distance to make the pass safely[33]

Ken taking the full lane

Some motorists, some police, and even some courts are of the erroneous belief that cyclists must **always** ride as far to the right as possible. This is simply not true.

## CAN WE RIDE TWO ABREAST?

Cyclists can ride two abreast on the road (unless riding on a path or part of a road reserved for the exclusive use of bicycles, in which case you may ride more than two abreast).[34] A very small minority of local ordinances still exist that prohibit riding two abreast, but a local law should generally give way to the ORC when it fundamentally conflicts, and the ORC explicitly **permits** riding two abreast. Conversely, a local ordinance providing **broader** cyclist rights that conflicts with the ORC would also be invalid. (*Kane v. City of Dayton* in Chapter Ten provides an example.)

# CAN WE BE FORCED TO RIDE ON SIDEWALKS? IS IT EVEN LEGAL TO MAKE US DO SO?!

As previously mentioned, **cyclists in Ohio can't be forced to ride on a sidewalk by a local authority or municipality**.[35] Some cities, such as Columbus, allow children under the age of 10 to ride on them, but make it illegal for everyone else.[36] Cincinnati allows minors under the age of 15 to ride on sidewalks under certain circumstances.[37] The National Highway Transportation Safety Administration (NHTSA) agrees, and states in its "Bicycle Safety" publication that children under 10 are safer when cycling away from traffic because young children can't always make safe decisions when riding on the road unsupervised.[38]

**It is legal to ride on a sidewalk if not prohibited by a local ordinance**, yet municipalities can't force you to,[39] so be careful on sidewalks, and be aware of possible restrictions in your own local ordinances.

**Please note:** Per the ORC, even when sidewalk riding is allowed cyclists must yield to pedestrians, who legally have the right of way on sidewalks.[40] Many municipalities require an audible signal from a cyclist passing a pedestrian.[41]

# DO WE HAVE TO OBEY TRAFFIC CONTROL DEVICES?

In Ohio cyclists are presently bound by the same laws as motorists, including red lights and stop signs.[42 & 43 & 44 & 45] Some other states have more liberal laws concerning cyclist duties at these traffic control devices (see Chapter Four) but at the time of writing, Ohio does not, barring an important exception. (See more regarding Ohio's "Dead Red light" later in this chapter under Newer Bike Laws Protecting Ohio Cyclists.)

Cleveland's first bike signal downtown on the Veterans Memorial
(Detroit-Superior) Bridge

Cleveland's first cyclist-specific traffic light (pictured here, and on book cover) has been installed downtown. It features individual lights in the shape of bicycles and, following the usual pattern of green/yellow/red, provides for safer navigation of one of Cleveland's busy intersections along one of its priority bicycle corridors.

This make sense because cyclist compliance with traffic control devices goes way up when bike specific infrastructure like bike signals is present. When Chicago added a protected lane and bike-specific traffic signals to Dearborn Street, stoplight compliance of bicycles quickly rose from 31 to 81 percent. If you build it, they will comply.[46]

# AND, ABOUT THOSE HAND SIGNALS...

Predictability is an important factor for cyclist safety. When practical, a cyclist should try to avoid erratic movements or excessive weaving. Cyclists should try to announce their turns and stops with state-mandated hand signals[47] which I demonstrate here, and which don't have to be held continuously,[48] aren't necessary in turn lanes, and don't need to be given if it will interfere with the safe operation of the bike, e.g., if the rider is uncomfortable taking a hand off the handlebars.

Turning left: left hand and arm extended horizontally

Turning right: left hand and arm extended upward (the "old school" right turn signal),
OR right hand and arm extended horizontally (the "modern" right turn signal)
NOTE: Although both are legal, the "old school right" (pictured above) may be
confusing to younger motorists

Stopping, or decreasing speed: right hand and arm extended downward

# WHEN DO I NEED TO USE LIGHTS ON MY BIKE?

The ORC mandates that our bikes have specific, activated front white lights and red rear lights at **night (sunset to**

**sunrise).**[49] No legal requirement exists in Ohio to have these activated lights on during the **day,** unless visibility is less than 1,000 feet due to atmospheric conditions (e.g., fog) or when windshield wiper use is necessary on motor vehicles (e.g., rain). In addition to a rear light, the ORC also requires you have a red rear reflector unless your light is capable of performing this function as well.[50] Cyclists should try to be prepared with these lights in case they end up riding at dusk or dawn, or during rainy or foggy periods with low visibility.

Some cyclists choose to activate daytime running lights in an attempt to increase visibility. This is a personal choice, not a legal requirement. As previously mentioned, the 2020 pandemic created somewhat of a bicycle boom of new riders, and I've seen many people on the streets without lights on at sundown! All riders, experienced or new, should be aware that Ohio law requires bike lights at night.

# MUST I WEAR A HELMET?!

As of June 2020, no federal law exists making bike helmets a requirement. Ohio law doesn't require adults to wear bike helmets, but at the time of writing **24 cities** in Ohio require them for minors (including Lakewood), and if you live in Shaker Heights, a local law requires them for adults.[51]

The efficacy of wearing a bike helmet is the subject of much debate and is generally a **personal**, not a legal, choice for adults. Some cyclists don't want them, others can't afford them. We don't want the State mandating helmets because of equity concerns around affordability, and one argument is that it could result in potential police targeting of low-income people for unrelated reasons.

Nevertheless, with head injuries causing approximately three-quarters of cyclist fatalities and one review finding that with helmet use, the risk of brain or head injury in any kind of bike crash dropped by approximately two-thirds,[52] wearing a helmet is something to consider. Bike club etiquette generally calls for wearing one, and many local group rides will not allow you to join the ride without one.

Serious, long-lasting head/brain injuries can and do occur. Advancements in helmet technology like "Multi-Directional Impact Protection System" ("MIPS", first available in 2010)[53] and "WaveCel" (released in 2019)[54] claim to reduce head injuries and increase favorable outcomes. How much better or effective these newer helmets are, only time will tell, and it's important to remember that helmets are not a cure-all.

Concussions are common in bike crashes, with some injured cyclists suffering on-going, debilitating symptoms. It's a good idea to familiarize yourself with the symptoms of a concussion and post-concussion syndrome[55] which many cyclists develop after a head impact, even when wearing a helmet.

# WHAT ARE THE LAWS REGARDING STAYING VISIBLE WHILE CYCLING?

No legal "visibility requirement" exists for cyclists in Ohio—what people wear when they ride is also a matter of **personal**, not legal, choice. As cyclists we do not want the State or a local authority mandating the specifics of our cycling wardrobes. However, a practical suggestion for cyclists wanting to stay extra visible is to consider wearing reflective, fluorescent, bright, and/ or contrasting clothing. This also can be especially effective on rotating parts of your bike and clothing e.g., pedals, wheels, socks, and shoes.

Since it's not legally mandated in Ohio, no defense exists for any cyclist's personal decision or financial inability to purchase or wear such clothing. In other words, if an unsafe motorist hits a cyclist, the motorist has no legal defense that the cyclist "could've or should've been wearing brighter clothing". That would be akin to arguing that a motor vehicle that was smashed into from behind should've been painted in bright or neon colors!

# CAN CYCLISTS GET TRAFFIC TICKETS?

When cycling, **we can be ticketed, but no Bureau of Motor Vehicles (BMV) points can be assessed on our driver's licenses—unless it's a driving under the influence (DUI) situation!**[56] If you drink above the legal limit and then ride, you'll risk getting a DUI with all the points and suspensions applicable to a driver of a motor vehicle **and** the added penalty of a non-expungable offense.

Never waive a bike traffic ticket unless you are sure that **no points** will be assessed on your driver's license. Believe me, cyclists often get BMV points because some courts, some prosecutors, and even some police don't know that points **cannot** be assessed for a bike traffic ticket that isn't a DUI.

# NEWER BIKE LAWS
# PROTECTING OHIO CYCLISTS

Ohio is making real progress regarding laws that protect us as cyclists!

**Three-Foot Passing Law:** This is Ohio's statewide three-foot minimum safe distance passing requirement. Drivers of motor vehicles must allow for at least three feet between their vehicle and a cyclist, when passing. This law became effective March 21, 2017.[57] Again, check your local ordinances for variations. For example—Cleveland has a six-foot passing ordinance for commercial trucks.[58]

One vehicle safely passing Ken with three feet of clearance

**Dead Red Exception:** Ohio's "dead red" exception permits a cyclist at a red light to stop, then safely enter the intersection on "dead red" which occurs **only** when a red light malfunctions/doesn't trip to green when failing to detect a bicycle's presence (many intersections only detect motor vehicles). The cyclist

**must** make sure it is safe to go, since the cyclist **won't** have the right of way because the oncoming traffic light will still be green! This law also became effective March 21, 2017.[59]

**This is not a law that allows cyclists to proceed through red lights unimpeded.** Don't become a "dead" red statistic by misinterpreting this law!

# 3

# ROAD SITUATIONS & ISSUES ENCOUNTERED BY CYCLISTS

T his chapter offers an overview of situations and issues we cyclists encounter—from legally navigating turns, intersections, sidewalks, and other bike infrastructure—to handling sticky situations that sometimes come up on our roadways.

# HOW DO I MAKE A LEFT TURN IN OHIO?

§4511.36(A)(2)[60] states:

*At any intersection where traffic is permitted to move in both directions on each roadway entering the intersection, an approach for a left turn shall be made in that portion of the right half of the roadway nearest the center line thereof and by passing to the right of such center line where it enters the intersection and after entering the intersection the left turn shall be made so as to leave the intersection to the right of the center line of the roadway being entered. Whenever practicable the left turn shall be made in that portion of the intersection to the left of the center of the intersection.*

This is the same basic process used when driving a motor vehicle. When turning at an intersection in which traffic is traveling in both directions, as cyclists, we need to make the turn from the lane nearest the center line. Once we begin the left turn, we must stay to the right of the center line of the road we're entering. Before turning, remember to try to use a left hand turn signal at some point if you can do so without jeopardizing your safety (unless in a designated turning lane).

It requires a little forethought, but when cycling we should try to prepare for making left turns by gradually moving into the lane closest to the center line as we approach the intersection. If you feel comfortable and safe doing so, a hand signal may help you to merge left, in order to get into position to make the left hand turn. The sooner we anticipate the merge, the easier it is to maneuver to the left lane (or, if there is only one lane in that direction, the left portion of the lane we are in) from which we'll be turning.[61] Once the turn is complete, we should then start cycling toward the right half of the lane, easing into the far right lane if one exists. Remember to try to use the left turn signal unless you are in a turn only lane or unless it will interfere with your safe bike operation. The signal doesn't have to be held continuously.

# HOW DO I MAKE A RIGHT TURN IN OHIO?

§4511.36(A)(1)[62] states:

*Approach for a right turn and a right turn shall be made as close as practicable to the right-hand curb or edge of the roadway.*

At an intersection, to make a lawful right turn in Ohio, we must ride our bikes to the right of the lane as close as is "practicable" to the curb on the right side, or to the edge of the road. This statute is vague, in that it refers to the curb **or** the edge. Try to make a right turn from the safest turning point on the road lane to the right. Cyclists turning right should try to give a right hand turn signal at some point before or during the right turn, unless in a right turn only lane or it interferes with the safe operation of their bicycle. The signal doesn't have to be held continuously.

## BIKE BOXES

To help mitigate the drama involved for cyclists turning left, bike infrastructure (known as "bike boxes") is being installed in cities across the U.S. According to the National Association of City Transportation Officials (NACTO)[63] a bike box is "a designated area at the head of a traffic lane at a signalized intersection that provides bicyclists with a safe and visible way to get ahead of queuing traffic during the red signal phase."

A "two-stage bike box" is a little different and helps people on bikes make left turns without having to make an unnerving left movement in busy traffic—to make a "normal left." Essentially, a two-stage bike box creates a space for cyclists to get across an intersection, stop, position themselves facing left, wait for the light to change, and then proceed. This sequence looks a lot like a pedestrian crossing the street, waiting for the next light to change then crossing again, only it's all done on a bike and with the right of way.

With bike boxes, groups of cyclists can move through intersections and crosswalks more quickly, minimizing wait time for motor vehicles, public transit vehicles, and pedestrians. As of this writing, two-stage bike boxes can be found in Cleveland at both the eastern and western ends of the Veterans Memorial (Detroit-Superior) Bridge.

Downtown Cleveland Bike Box

# REGARDING BIKES AND INTERSECTIONS...

NACTO published its *Urban Bikeway Design Guide* back in 2011.[64] Since then, the mileage of protected bike lanes across North America has increased over 600%! While this statistic is impressive, it has also highlighted the need for better intersection design. Of all urban cycling fatalities in 2017, 43% of them happened at intersections.[65] NACTO's new report released in May 2019 and titled *Don't Give Up at the Intersection* includes information illustrating how design factors like lane width and turning radii can affect motorist decisions. The wider the lane and the larger the turn radius, the easier it is for a driver of a motor vehicle to make a fast "sweeping" turn, which makes intersections more dangerous for people on bikes and on foot.[66] Generally, if motorists are given too much space, they will use it to speed without even thinking about it, and this is why good street design is critical.

# WHAT IS A "SHARROW"? HOW DO ROADS OR LANES WITH SHARROWS DIFFER FROM DESIGNATED BIKE LANES?

Shared Lane Marking (Sharrow)

A Shared Lane Marking or "**sharrow**" is an image of two chevrons above a bicycle logo that is painted onto the street. Though similar to a bike lane symbol to the untrained eye, sharrows are typically **used in shared-use travel lanes (think regular streets) of 35 mph or less and do not set aside specific space for bicycles.** This author agrees with Bike Cleveland's position that a street with a sharrow painted on it doesn't comprise a complete bicycle facility when used alone. Sharrows are best used in conjunction with other road treatments like "Bicycles May Use Full Lane" signage, when the speed limit is **preferably at or below 25 mph,** and only on streets where a better type of facility or road treatment isn't feasible.

Theoretically a sharrow has several functions, potentially helping cyclists to:

- Position themselves correctly in the lane

- Avoid "dooring" collisions, which happen when a motorist opens their vehicle door into an oncoming cyclist; sharrows are eleven feet from the curb in areas with on-street parking, and four feet from the curb where there's no parking

- Be regarded as legit/legal by other road users; when a sharrow reminds motorists that cyclists are on the road, it can help foster better understanding between the two groups, and help reduce aggression because a motorist who is anticipating encountering cyclists will theoretically handle the encounter better when they are not startled or fearful

The first sharrows in Cleveland were added in May 2008 along Franklin Avenue on Cleveland's near-west side.[67]

# BIKE LANES

Designated Bike Lane with Dooring Zone markings in Lakewood, Ohio

Striped bike lanes—perhaps the most common form of easily recognizable bicycle infrastructure—are usually two solid painted lines near the right edge of a street and include a bike lane symbol (a painted bicycle accompanied with a solid arrow pointing in the direction of travel). You will find these all over the country, and for many bicycle advocates they constitute the minimum acceptable level of bike infrastructure.

Designated bike lanes are generally much preferred over shared use lanes marked with sharrows because they **reserve specific space for people to ride bikes**, whereas sharrows, without providing any separation, merely help people understand that bikes also may use regular travel lanes.[68]

A Cleveland municipal ordinance provides that cyclists have the right of way when riding in a designated bicycle lane. Motor vehicles shall not and cannot drive in any bike lane, or otherwise place a vehicle in a bike lane, in a way that could impede bicycle traffic including parking in one. Motorists may still **briefly** cross bike lanes to make turns, access parking, and to enter or exit the roadway, but these exceptions only apply when the bike lane is clear of any bike traffic.[69]

Protected Bike Lane in Cleveland with bollards/delineators

**Did I mention that parking in bike lanes is not allowed in Cleveland?** No vehicle can stand or be parked in a bike lane except for a bicycle.[70]

# WHAT ABOUT AGGRESSIVE MOTORIST BEHAVIOR LIKE HONKING OR YELLING?

Many, if not most cyclists have been honked at by impatient motorists who likely think there's no rule against it, and who are upset with us for exercising our legal right to ride on the road. However, "unnecessary sounding of horns" **is** prohibited in Cleveland's municipal code.[71]

It's important to remember that most motorists are courteous and pass without incident, but any cyclist will tell you they routinely experience verbal hostility and even physical intimidation from drivers of motor vehicles unhappy with our presence. The hostility is lessening, thankfully!

# 4

# FOR THE
# MOTORIST
## WHY WE CYCLISTS DO WHAT WE DO!

# WHAT THE **** IS
# THAT CYCLIST DOING?!

This section is for the motorists' understanding. As we all know, misunderstanding can sometimes create the wrong idea. For instance, bike maneuvers that appear illogical to a motorist may have a perfectly valid reason for occurring.

A word of caution about this section: what follows you may disagree with, and the actions you read about may not be entirely legal **yet may be entirely practical**. We pause from the legal theme for a moment to address some real-world bike behavior that you've likely already witnessed and lend a perspective that might help you understand **why** you're seeing it. The idea is that a little more understanding might foster a little more patience. Why do we seek this? Because everyone wants to get home safely no matter what vehicle they're operating. To that end, the following is some behavior you might see displayed by your two-wheeled cousins of the road, and why they do it.

## WHY ARE THOSE CYCLISTS RIDING IN A PACK LIKE THAT? THEY'RE TAKING UP THE WHOLE ROAD!

It's easy to forget how nearly effortless it seems to cruise along at 25+ mph in your motor vehicle. In fact, it often feels downright slow traveling at that speed, even though 25 mph is the upper limit on a significant number of our roads. Strong cyclists can cruise along at, or near this speed but most can't.

Did you know that wind is the cause of roughly 80% of the resistance a bike rider feels while on their bike? This is where group riding comes in! That's right, drafting isn't just for NASCAR[72]—it's just as important in cycling. On average (depending on the speed) it takes roughly one-quarter less effort and energy to maintain a speed above 20 mph if another rider is blocking the wind by riding in front of you. The faster you go, the greater the effect.[73] This is the main reason you see those *Tour de France*[74] types riding in a single line almost on top of each other; the leader who is "pulling" is taking the brunt of the wind, allowing the others to use less energy while matching his or her speed in their draft.

Because the lead rider is taking all the wind, they tend to get tired more quickly and need to take a break, so all the riders in the group typically take turns swapping off as leader, allowing the group as a whole to maintain a speed that may otherwise be unattainable for any individual rider.

Sometimes, particularly in places like the Cleveland Metroparks,[75] you'll find groups of four, six, eight, or more cyclists drafting like this in a double file configuration. Some people's first thought is that they're blocking the lane, but when you see this, you should understand that it's far easier and safer for a motorist to pass a compact group of riders rolling along two abreast than it is to pass the same number of riders in a single long line. If you're passing safely, the shorter the overall line of riders, the shorter the time you spend alongside them while facing oncoming traffic.

As a motorist, what should you do? Be patient, wait for a clear sight line, and pass the group of cyclists the same as you would pass any other slow-moving vehicle like a bus or a buggy. A group such as this is aware of your presence, likely will have verbally alerted the rest of the group by shouting "car back" or "passing" and is wanting you to be out of that position on the road as much as you do!

## STOP SIGNS AND GROUP RIDING

As for groups of cyclists going through stop signs together, riding through one by one would hold things up for motorists and drive everyone crazy. Again, not 100% legal, but it's a courtesy to all out in traffic when the cyclists stop and start as a whole group. In a well-known 2015 protest, cyclists in San Francisco responded to a police crackdown against their "rolling" stop signs by doing precisely what the law prescribes: individual riders each coming to a full and complete stop at the stop signs on a popular urban route called The Wiggle. The results were predictably chaotic, with motorists blaring horns and yelling because of the delay caused by the increased congestion created when people on bikes followed a law that was promulgated for motor vehicles.[76]

Finally, a motorist might encounter a group of cyclists and without even thinking about it, begin to overtake them regardless if it's safe for oncoming traffic, themselves, or the cyclists. This is common in the Cleveland Metroparks which has multiple blind corners. A motorist should never pass a group of cyclists unless they can do so safely without exceeding the speed limit.[77] Never pass a group of cyclists on a blind curve!

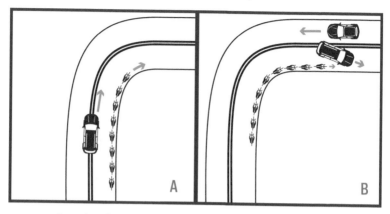

Examples of motorists unsafely passing cyclists on blind curves

Even when an oncoming motorist, lawfully in their lane with the right of way, is facing a motor vehicle on the wrong side of the road unsafely passing a group of cyclists (as in illustration B), this lawful motorist should still try to **get out of the way** by moving to the right and letting the oncoming vehicle safely pass all the cyclists. The cyclists are not doing anything wrong, yet they may be the ones most at risk if the motor vehicles collide! Also, when passing a cyclist or group of cyclists, watch out for oncoming cyclists!

# WHY DO CYCLISTS POINT AT THE ROAD?

There's one other very common signal you'll see cyclists perform when you encounter a group: pointing rather deliberately at the ground. What are they pointing at? Usually potholes, but it could be any surface hazard. What feels like merely a jarring pothole in your motor vehicle would almost certainly cause a bike rider to crash if they were to hit it. How do cyclists deal with this reality when they're in a group? The lead riders point out surface hazards so the rest of the group can avoid them.

Hazard hand signal

# A CYCLIST IS STANDING ON BOTH PEDALS, BUT THEY SEEM STOPPED . . . WHAT'S UP WITH THAT?

When a cyclist is standing balanced on their pedals while stopped at a red light, they're "track standing." This position of readiness for the experienced cyclist allows them to start moving again more quickly when the light changes. Admittedly, this can be confusing to motorists, especially those who aren't also cyclists. While it's an advanced skill for a cyclist it may be better if they make their intention of stopping clearer by putting at least one foot on the ground.

## "FILTERING"

You have likely seen this as well. A cyclist will ride up the side of traffic queued at a red light and position themselves at the front of the line. Absent a bike lane, cyclists are generally supposed to wait in line like a motor vehicle, but there are practical reasons for filtering. Specifically, some cyclists think they are more visible positioned at the front of the line rather than being "buried" in a line of much larger vehicles that can obscure the cyclist's presence. By being first and anticipating when the light changes, the cyclist may be able to clear the intersection more quickly in a more visible manner, which may be safer for the cyclist given the high crash rates at those locations.

# I DON'T SEE THAT STUFF MUCH . . . I SEE CYCLISTS JUMPING LIGHTS AND STOP SIGNS, AND IT MAKES ME MAD.

We could cite the statistics showing that people break the law on the roads at similar rates regardless of the vehicle they choose, but that isn't the point of this section. By no means do we condone illegal conduct. We're merely attempting to shed light on **why** such behavior exists. Even though bikes are supposed to be co-equal vehicles under the law, traffic engineers have historically ignored cyclists and share some of the blame in creating an environment where cyclists feel marginalized and not part of the system. And what do people do when they don't feel like they're a part of something? They may ignore some of the rules and defining characteristics of that system. We need to build a more inclusive system with rules better designed for people on bikes. Other places in the United States are already doing so.

Idaho lawmakers first legalized the "Idaho Stop" in 1982—the first law in the United States allowing cyclists to treat stop signs as "yields" and red lights as stop signs—and cycling advocates as well as cities and states around the country have endorsed these ideas. A cyclist has a much better vantage point from a traffic control device like a red light or a stop sign than that of a motorist. In 2017 the State of Delaware approved a variation applying only to stop signs and referred to as the "Delaware Yield". The Idaho Stop legislation was also passed in the Utah House of Representatives yet as of this writing hasn't passed in the state Senate. Cities including San Francisco have contemplated yet ultimately decided against it, which is a shame considering that just one year after its passage Idaho saw a 14% drop in bicycle injuries and, fast-forwarding 28 years, ranked 30% better than "comparable peers" regarding bike safety. As of this writing, Arkansas was the third state to add a version of the Idaho Stop to their laws in April 2019,[78] followed by Oregon in June 2019[79] and Washington in March 2020.[80] This author hopes Ohio considers such legislation in the future.

# 5

# MOTORIST RESPONSIBILITIES: DISTRACTED DRIVING & DOORING

**H**umans are territorial and instinctual by nature. Motorists focus on their destinations and loathe obstructions and delays. A minority of them openly detest cyclists, to the point of absurdly suggesting that an injured or killed cyclist "got what they deserved" for riding on the road, even though a cyclist's right to do so is authorized and sanctioned by Ohio Law.

# DISTRACTED DRIVING

People who ride after dark or commute know how scary it is to see the "glowing faces" of people behind the wheels of their motor vehicles, the illumination caused by their cellphone screens while they are obviously looking down at their phones rather than devoting their full attention to the act of driving. Bike crashes are often the result of motorists driving while distracted: texting, talking on cell phones, emailing, even watching movies while behind the wheel! Phone use in general creates dangerous issues for cyclists around motorists. This modern phone usage is much more dangerous than merely talking on the phone because the person texting is literally looking down or otherwise taking their eyes off the road. It has become such an issue it's being referred to as the "new drunk driving"[81] and safety officials are increasingly aware:

- A 2019 report by the National Transportation Safety Board calls for eliminating distractions as a "most wanted" safety improvement and calls for banning all personal electronic device use on our roadways throughout the nation[82]

- According to the Ohio Department of Transportation (ODOT), between 2013 and 2017 there were nearly 66,000 crashes in Ohio due to distracted driving[83]

# CURRENT DISTRACTED DRIVING LAWS

Ohio law currently prohibits texting or emailing while driving (with a few exceptions).[84] For minors on a temporary/probationary driver's license, this prohibition extends to cell phone use more generally, not just texting.[85] In October 2018, Ohio House Bill 95 went into effect "enhancing" the moving-violation-while-driving-distracted penalty. How? If law enforcement believes that a motorist is distracted while committing a moving violation, and the distraction is a contributing factor to the moving violation, the motorist is subject to an additional fine. This Ohio statute makes distracted driving a "secondary" offense, not a "primary" offense. That means that, at the time of writing, a police officer cannot pull you over for using your cell phone independently of another "primary" violation (like speeding or failing to obey a traffic control device). A first violation will result in a misdemeanor.[86]

# THE PUSH FOR PRIMARY

Ohio is moving toward making distracted driving a primary offense, meaning that a police officer could cite a motorist who is distracted yet not committing any other traffic offense. Some cities have already written this into law. In September 2019, the City of Lakewood passed new legislation making driving while using a cell phone (aside from hands-free) or another electronic wireless communication device a primary offense.[87]

Research has shown that spending a mere five seconds texting—the amount of time the average text takes to send—at 55 mph, is the equivalent of driving a football field's entire length **with your eyes closed!**[88]

The Ohio Bicycle Federation (OBF) is working toward making distracted driving a primary offense in Ohio.[89] Gov. Mike DeWine believes that distracted driving ". . . should be as culturally unacceptable as drunk driving is today," and announced in April 2019 that a permanent Distracted Driving Advisory Council is now in place to "develop" a longstanding plan to "change the culture" around this issue.[90] Distracted driving is well on its way to becoming a primary offense in Ohio, and this is an important step in improving safety for all road users regardless of how they use them.

On January 14, 2020—after communicating throughout 2019 with Sharon Montgomery, a constituent whose life was impacted tragically in 2000 when she and her husband John were in a crash caused by a distracted motorist[91] whose only penalty was a $75 fine—State Rep. Mary Lightbody (D-Westerville) introduced House Bill 468 for safer roads in Ohio.[92] This legislation, which Ms. Montgomery helped to develop, was the first step toward making driving a motor vehicle while using a handheld electronic device a primary offense for all Ohioans.

Making distracted driving a primary offense, like a DUI offense, is also a rising national trend.[93] Clearly, distracted driving can be just as deadly as driving under the influence. Besides texting (non-hands-free), distracted driving includes any activity not necessary to operating a vehicle, which impairs the ability of the motorist to drive safely e.g., taking their eyes off the road to pick up something off the vehicle floor.

Additionally, on February 13, 2020, the "Hands Free Ohio" bill was announced by Gov. Mike DeWine.[94]

# DOORING

"Dooring", a growing issue for cyclists and motorists, occurs when a motorist in a parked vehicle opens their driver's side door without first checking to see if anyone (such as a cyclist) is passing on the left. One way to ensure safe door opening is to employ a strategy originating in the Netherlands and known as the "Dutch Reach." When parking a motor vehicle and preparing to exit, reaching across the body to open the driver's side door with the **right** hand rather than the left causes the body to pivot, providing an automatic view of the blind spot and who/what might be coming along the road from behind.

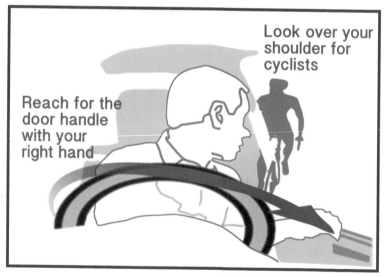

The Ohio Revised Code states that no person shall open the door on the side available to moving traffic unless, and until it is **reasonably safe** and can be done **without interfering** with the **movement** of other **traffic.** Violation of this statute results in a minor misdemeanor and a fine of up to $150[95] and on top of that, you may be civilly liable to an injured cyclist. And attention, cyclists: If you are in a dooring crash caused by an unsafe motorist, be sure to get that motorist's drivers license, license plate and insurance info, just as you would if involved in any other bike crash! While the adrenaline is pumping, you might not realize the extent of your injuries.

The point here is that it's incumbent upon motorists to ensure that it's 100% safe when opening their driver's side doors. So, why not give the Dutch Reach a try? Then, share it with everyone you know who drives a motor vehicle!

# 6

# BIKE
# CRASHES
AWARENESS, CONSEQUENCES & PREVENTION

**E**ven though I talk about crashes in this book, cycling is generally safe in Ohio when you look at the number of people cycling versus the number of injuries. However, bike crashes do occur, and there isn't always a protected bike lane available, so it is worth mentioning that those who practice "vehicular cycling"—i.e., riding their bike like they drive their motor vehicle—are in 75-80% fewer crashes! Awareness on the part of both motorists and cyclists can go a long way in helping to prevent bike/auto crashes. Riding your bike in this manner usually gives a cyclist the right of way, or the right to proceed uninterruptedly.

## CAUSES AND TYPES OF BIKE CRASHES

Among the numerous types of bike crashes caused by unsafe motorists, a few of them happen so frequently they have names:

- The Rear Ender: Just how it sounds, a **motor vehicle** crashes into a **cyclist** from behind

- The Left Cross: A **motor vehicle** turns left, directly in front of an oncoming **cyclist**

- The Right Hook, Part 1: A **motor vehicle** passes a **cyclist**, then turns right directly in front of the **cyclist**

- The Right Hook, Part 2: A **cyclist** on the right is passing a slower-moving or stopped **motor vehicle** on the cyclist's left, and the **motor vehicle** suddenly turns directly into the **cyclist**

You'll notice that all of these are turning maneuvers which highlight intersections as places requiring extra care.

# WHAT SHOULD A MOTORIST DO TO AVOID A BIKE CRASH?

It's simple, motorists **should** remain aware and be on the lookout for people on bikes, not just for people in motor vehicles, and **shouldn't drive distractedly!** Motorists should also realize that **bicycles are legal road vehicles with the right of way, so when you're pulling out of your driveway, wait for a bike to safely pass, as you would for any other vehicle with the right of way.**

## WHAT SHOULD A CYCLIST DO?

Cyclists should also remain aware and be on the lookout for other road users. Beyond that, and particularly around intersections, if cycling on a street that's too narrow for a motor vehicle to safely pass a cyclist, the cyclist may consider taking the full (whole) lane by moving toward the center of the lane—this could help to prevent anyone in a motor vehicle from passing too closely to the cyclist on the left or potentially right-hooking them. Moreover, an oncoming, left-turning motorist may have a clearer view of the approaching cyclist because the cyclist is positioned where motorists typically look for other motor vehicles.

Ken taking the full lane

# ALL PURPOSE TRAILS IN THE METROPARKS AND CVNP

If you're riding on the all purpose trail in the Metroparks or Cuyahoga Valley National Park (CVNP), try to get off the trail when stopping or if having an issue with your bike. Be careful to look for oncoming cyclists if riding double, and if you **are** riding double move out of the way of an oncoming cyclist. Obey the center line of the trail if one is present, and if not, treat the trail as if it has an imaginary center line and don't cross over unless it's safe. Be especially careful not to cross over on a blind curve with potential oncoming cyclists. Try to announce your intentions when passing i.e., "Passing on the left" or "Riders passing on the left" if you're first to pass in a group.

# THE "STOBBE SHOUT"

Gary Stobbe and I grew up together on Cleveland's west side. He drove a '68 Chevy with no working horn. (Back in the day, motor vehicles often had numerous things wrong with them.) In situations which called for honking, often Gary would simply shout, and other motorists would actually hear him and stop. Thus, to me, the "Stobbe Shout" was born.

Gary Stobbe 2020

This method can be as useful today as it was in the 70s! While cycling recently in Florida—which has a huge retirement population—I would often resort to a "Stobbe Shout" to "wake up" a motorist from their inattention. Things happen quickly on the road, and depending on the situation, the Stobbe Shout (or a verbal or bell alert of some kind) could be useful. However, this is obviously not a legal requirement by any means. This is merely a tactic a cyclist may employ.

# 7

# CYCLIST HIT BY AN UNSAFE MOTORIST

## IMPORTANT STEPS TO TAKE

Thereusually isn't much warning before a crash, so adopt the Boy Scouts of America's motto and "Be Prepared!"[96]

Beyond maintaining awareness, an important part of our duty as cyclists is to have **a plan for coping with a crash**, should one unfortunately occur. To that end I've created a handy acronym: "P.H.O.N.E.":

**P** is for **Police**: Call the police and insist on a report, **no matter what**; you need documentation! **Always** call the police, even if the motorist begs you not to and/or seems like a saint or even if the police try to talk you out of filing a report! If you don't, the lack of a record and documentation of the crash will cause you later suffering!

**H** is for **Healthcare**: Seek immediate medical attention for **all** injuries.

**O** is for **Observe/Obtain**: Get the motorist's contact and insurance info, and names of all witnesses, or try to make sure the police or other witnesses or bystanders obtain this vital information.

**N** is for **Notification**: Call an experienced bike injury attorney **before** you talk to the at fault motorist's liability adjuster. The adjusters are pros for the insurance companies—hire a pro for yourself! Remember, the liability adjuster for the motorist is **not** on your side. It's in their insurance company's best interest to pressure you for information and into **agreeing to terms that may not even come close to covering all damages**. Never sign or agree to sign a settlement before consulting with an attorney, because you may be inadvertently waiving your right to pursue legal action to recover the full amount for your injuries and you may have to live with your rash decision for the rest of your life. One good example is the case of *Bailey v. Vaughn*, 2017-Ohio-7725 (Ct. App.) in which an unrepresented injury victim was stuck with a paltry settlement which he accepted from the liability insurance company before he got his own lawyer.

**E** is for **Evidence**: After a crash, try to be your own legal reporter and document in detail all you can see and recall until police arrive on the scene. Don't let the at fault party move their motor vehicle **or** your bicycle before the police arrive. Look for a building security camera that may have recorded the crash. Be sure to keep all damaged property (without cleaning or repairing it) including, for example, the bike frame, ripped clothing and accessories, and make sure you check the inside and outside of your helmet for cracks or other signs of head impact that may not be remembered or apparent to you in the moments after a crash. These items are **valuable pieces of evidence**. In the moments after being hit this can be particularly difficult, but if you're able, this is an important step.

If you have a modern GPS-enabled bicycle computer like a Garmin or a Wahoo, check the data for the actual speed and location of where the crash took place, and let your attorney know if you have ride footage from a GoPro-type camera.[97] These cameras, along with non-mandated daytime lights, are a growing trend among cyclists as they take additional steps in an attempt to protect themselves. Tell your attorney if you are on Strava or MapMyRide or a similar app so your ride information can be downloaded.

Knabe Law Firm[98] has **a supply of laminated P.H.O.N.E. business cards** you can easily carry in your pocket to help you remember the important steps to take in the event of a crash. Please contact our office to request a complementary card be mailed to you. The reverse side of these cards lists a "**Cyclist's Arsenal**" with current Ohio bike laws that all cyclists should have at their fingertips while out on the road.

**Time is of the essence after a crash.** Time gaps between the crash and your seeking medical or legal services can have an impact on your recovery. As soon as possible, contact an experienced personal injury attorney who specializes in bike crashes. Legal services are like medical services in this regard. If you have a specific medical condition you don't only see a general practitioner—you make an appointment with a specialist. When it comes to bikes and the law, that's me. Finally, consider using your cell phone to photograph the crash location, location of your bike and the motor vehicle that hit you, and your injuries. You can also take pictures of the motorist's driver's license and insurance info.

# 8

# DAMAGES IN A BIKE/AUTO CRASH

MORE THAN YOU MIGHT THINK!

BIKE AND ACCESSORY DAMAGES

ECONOMIC DAMAGES: MEDICAL/LOST WAGES

NON-ECONOMIC DAMAGES: PAIN/SUFFERING/DISABILITY

CLEVELAND CYCLIST ASHLEY SHAW'S STORY

P hysical injuries are often the first thing we think of after a bike crash. A cyclist on a 15- to 50-pound bike **never** wins in a crash with a 2,000-pound box! Injuries are serious and no laughing matter, but as the old joke goes, "What about the bike?!"

# BIKE AND ACCESSORY DAMAGE

Property and accessory damage are almost guaranteed in any bike crash. Bikes aren't mere toys and can cost thousands of dollars! A damaged bike frame, wheel set, components, and accessories are often costly, and damage to these items can be **critically important evidence**. Not to mention the expensive smartphone you're likely carrying. A reputable bike shop will help in establishing fair dollar value for bike, components, and accessory damages. Most liability insurance carriers will pay a bike property damage claim if the estimates are accurate and backed up by photos.

To make an uninsured motorist claim in Ohio (that is, a claim against your own auto policy because the other party was uninsured) you need independent corroborative evidence of a hit-and-run crash. In addition to an eyewitness, the bike frame damage may constitute that evidence. Check the frame for paint transfer stains from the hit-and-run motorist's vehicle.

# ECONOMIC & NON-ECONOMIC DAMAGES: MEDICAL/LOST WAGES AND PAIN/SUFFERING/DISABILITY

In addition to compensation for bike component and accessory damage, injured cyclists are entitled to **separate sums** for both **economic**, and **non-economic** damages. Allow me to explain.

**Economic losses/damages** generally consist of past and future medical bills and loss of income. This is normally easy to calculate using simple math.

**Non-economic losses** are more nebulous to calculate because they include things like "pain and suffering". Pain is the neurological response to physical injury to the body, and **suffering** is psychological, meaning a mental or emotional state brought on by the injury such as nervousness, grief, anxiety, worry, shock, humiliation and indignity. **Basic losses** include the inability to perform the daily activities of life like walking, lifting, climbing stairs, feeding oneself, or driving. **Pleasurable losses** include the inability to engage in activities that a person enjoyed prior to the injury like cycling and other recreational activities, hobbies, and sports. Non-economic damages have a cap in Ohio, but these caps do not apply if you suffer a permanent, substantial injury or deformity.

Substantial injuries including broken bones and other serious, long-lasting physical injuries can occur when cyclists are hit by motor vehicles. Concussions are common even among those wearing helmets. Post-Concussion Syndrome can include dizziness, confusion, light sensitivity, noise sensitivity, headaches, memory loss and/or hearing loss. Traumatic Brain

Injuries occur all too frequently during bike crashes and can have an irreparable impact on a person's life. It's important to understand that while people often mistake concussions for a minor injury, they are much more serious. In his article, "An Overview of Traumatic Brain Injury," EMT-Paramedic Rod Brouhard states, "You can have TBI with or without a concussion, but you can't have a concussion without TBI."[99]

# CLEVELAND CYCLIST ASHLEY SHAW'S STORY

Ashley Shaw is a Cleveland resident living in Ohio City, a historic neighborhood on the near west side. In 2017, she was motor vehicle-free by choice and riding her bike a mere block from home when she was hit by a motor vehicle, causing her to sustain a TBI in the form of a subdural hematoma, a.k.a. a "brain bleed." She remembers only silence for the first several days after the crash, a silence that "will always stay with (her)."

For the first year after her crash, post-crash symptoms included noticeably slower speech and difficulty forming sentences, both verbally and in writing. She continues to experience short term memory loss, fatigue, nausea, light sensitivity, and issues with balance and falling. Perhaps most difficult of all is that despite appearing "healthy" to those around her, unseen symptoms of Post-Traumatic Stress Disorder (PTSD)[100] are part of her experience more often than not. Stressful situations—even simple everyday actions such as crossing a street—can be overwhelming, triggering her brain and sympathetic nervous system to activate the "fight-or-flight mode". In her own words, several times a day her body feels "as if it's being chased by a bear."

# ALL THIS, DUE TO A MOTORIST NOT PAYING ATTENTION BEHIND THE WHEEL.

Despite these ongoing challenges, Shaw has been able to move forward and currently serves as Director of Neighborhood Planning & Economic Development at Ohio City Incorporated,[101] as well as co-chair of the City of Cleveland's Vision Zero Enforcement Subcommittee. She's grateful for the opportunity this difficult life experience has offered her. In her own words:

*"Something really unexpected happens when you have a close call with your life. It puts the important things into perspective . . . I value my life, my experiences, and my relationships in a completely different way than I did before. My life now is simple and slow, but so much more meaningful. I am one of the lucky ones."*[102]

# 9

# INSURANCE
# FOR
# CYCLISTS

## HOW CAN INSURANCE PROTECT CYCLISTS?

## CAN I PURCHASE BIKE INSURANCE SEPARATELY FROM MY AUTO INSURANCE?

## SHOULD I CARRY AN UMBRELLA?!

## WHAT IF A CYCLIST HAS MINIMUM COVERAGE?

**D**ISCLAIMER: The information shared in this chapter is general. Each situation is uniquely fact based and each insurance policy is an individual contract, with specific language and exclusions varying from company to company.

## WHAT HAPPENS WHEN AN AT FAULT CYCLIST HITS A PEDESTRIAN OR MOTOR VEHICLE?

The cyclist is **not** covered under the cyclist's own auto liability policy; **but** the cyclist should be covered under the cyclist's own homeowner or renter policy per the liability section (as long as there are no written exclusions).

## WHAT HAPPENS WHEN A CYCLIST IS HIT BY AN AT FAULT MOTORIST WHO HAS NO LIABILITY INSURANCE COVERAGE?

The cyclist should be covered by the **uninsured** motorist protection under **the cyclist's own personal auto policy**, assuming the cyclist purchased this coverage known as "U **coverage**".

# WHAT HAPPENS WHEN A CYCLIST IS HIT BY AN AT FAULT MOTORIST WHO HAS INADEQUATE INSURANCE?

The cyclist should be covered under the cyclist's own **underinsured** (UIM) motorist protection in their personal auto policy; assuming the cyclist also has a motor vehicle for which they have purchased this coverage known as "**UIM coverage**" (as most cyclists also own motor vehicles). **For UIM to apply, the amount of the UIM coverage must exceed the liability limits of the at fault motorist's insurance policy.** U coverage and UIM coverage are typically combined in an auto policy under **U coverage,** so make sure to check your policy to confirm both U and UIM are counted in your policy under U coverage. **Remember, a cyclist doesn't have "full coverage" unless the cyclist has U coverage!**

These days, when folks are buying their auto insurance, they're often purchasing it online without professional advice. This is risky because all insurance coverage is simply not the same, and Ohio has eliminated the requirement of insurance companies offering certain coverages, including U coverage.

**The bottom line? Here is the coverage you should carry:**

- All cyclists whose budget can allow for it **should** purchase U coverage under their personal auto liability policy to protect them if they are hit by an at fault motorist with little, or no liability insurance; this coverage should also protect them if they are struck by a hit-and-run motorist, assuming there is independent corroborating evidence

- All cyclists should consider purchasing a homeowner or renter insurance policy that covers the cyclist's potential liability in injuring a person or damaging property; it also could cover bike theft and/or bike damage if you are hit by an at fault uninsured motorist

# CAN I PURCHASE BIKE INSURANCE SEPARATELY FROM MY AUTO INSURANCE?

**Cyclists with no homeowner, no renter, and/or no personal auto coverage** may consider purchasing a separate bicycle insurance policy. Check out "Velosurance" where you can obtain a quote and purchase a bicycle insurance policy online at velosurance.com.[103]

# SHOULD I CARRY AN UMBRELLA UNDER MY POLICY?

"Umbrella" insurance is typically insurance that covers liability claims in excess of your underlying auto or homeowner insurance limits. If you are at fault and injure someone, your liability umbrella coverage helps to prevent the injured party's collecting from your personal assets. Just as importantly for a cyclist, if it's offered, you should always elect U coverage under your umbrella policy to provide extra coverage if you're hit by an underinsured or uninsured motorist whose coverages are inadequate to compensate you.

# WHAT IF A CYCLIST HAS MINIMUM U COVERAGE?

Minimum coverage means minimum protection! You could run into trouble on your U coverage protection if you only have minimum coverage. Why? If your current U coverage is only $25,000 and the at fault motorist's liability coverage is $25,000, you can't collect more than $25,000 in insurance coverage no matter how badly you're hurt. Why? Because your own coverage matches that of the at fault motorist, so you only collect from theirs. It is better than nothing, but medical bills can quickly exceed this minimum amount.

**Remember**: you cannot depend on the at fault motorist to carry enough liability coverage to protect you. Be prepared and protect yourself, if your budget allows, by buying **full and adequate coverage**—not minimum coverage! We recommend at least $100,000/$300,000 in liability and U coverages, or more if your budget permits. We also recommend purchasing umbrella coverage which **could** provide extra liability and U coverage.

Some insurance companies are advertising minimum coverage "for the rest of us." This tells us that many motorists likely only have minimum coverage and offers further reason for cyclists to purchase higher amounts of UIM coverage themselves.

## WHAT ABOUT BIKE THEFT?

No cyclist wants to think about their bike getting stolen! However, if it happens, it's good to know that with most insurance companies your bike is covered under "personal property/contents" on your homeowner or renter policy, as long as it was taken from a known location. This coverage is subject to a deductible. If you've taken the extra step of "scheduling" your bike (scheduling means itemizing specific items of value to provide higher levels of protection), not only is it covered, you won't have to pay a deductible.

## WHAT ABOUT E-SCOOTER COVERAGE . . . OR LACK THEREOF?

E-scooters like the ones in downtown Cleveland provided by companies such as Bird and Lime are new. These companies know how to protect themselves—they require users to sign an agreement assuming full responsibility for anything happening during the time of use. In other words, if an e-scooter rider crashes into someone, they are personally responsible for that person's injuries. If a rider crashes into a tree, causing damage to the e-scooter, they are personally responsible for that damage. **The rider always bears full responsibility for liability for anything occurring during their ride.**

**The bottom line on scooter coverage:** if you choose to ride e-scooters, don't depend on the e-scooter companies to provide you with insurance coverage! Protect yourself in all possible ways. Make sure you have homeowner or renter insurance, which may cover you if you hit someone or something. Make sure you have U coverage under your auto policy, to cover you if you are hit by a motorist. And, check with your insurance agent about your coverage on e-scooters and other micro-mobility devices you may find yourself using.

# 10

# OHIO BIKE CASES

### REAL STUFF!

T he following are real Ohio bike cases, with real cyclists and real results. Read with care—you never know what may happen out on the road, but you **should** know what **could** happen!

*State v. Patrick, 914 N.E.2d 1121 (Ohio Mun. Ct. 2008)*[104]

Case type: CRIMINAL/TRAFFIC OFFENSES—CYCLIST

Two cyclists were allegedly riding two abreast when a police officer in a marked cruiser confronted them. The officer felt they were impeding traffic and attempted to stop them verbally and with lights and siren. The cyclists did not comply and the officer "tased" one of them. The tased cyclist faced criminal misdemeanor charges in Lawrence County Municipal Court—Resisting Arrest, Disorderly Conduct, Operating a Bicycle in the Roadway, and Failure to Comply with a Police Order.

The Lawrence County Municipal Court judge found the cyclist not guilty since he'd committed no violations and no probable cause of a crime existed for the officer's stopping him and his fellow cyclist. A local authority cannot prohibit cyclists from riding on the road unless it's a closed or limited access highway or freeway. Since the police orders were not lawful, no duty existed requiring the cyclist to halt, and he had a fundamental right under the Fourth Amendment (Amendment IV) to be left alone.

This is an interesting case and I'm glad the cyclist won. However, not all judges or juries are as knowledgeable or as sympathetic as this judge. Cyclists can ride two abreast in Ohio, and there is no requirement in the Ohio statute requiring cyclists to go single file to let traffic pass. That said, if a police officer orders you to stop it's often a good idea to comply, because getting charged and/or getting tased is not worth it. Just make sure you know the law and your rights.

As I mentioned earlier, to help with this, available at my office (and online at klfohio.com) are laminated P.H.O.N.E. bike cards containing all the laws that favor cyclists, including the right to ride two abreast! These free cards should be kept in your pocket or jersey on every ride and presented to any police officer who may be unaware of the evolving laws regarding bicycles and cyclist rights.

*State v. Gatto, 2007-Ohio-4609 (Ct. App.)*[105]

Case type: CRIMINAL OFFENSE—CYCLIST

A fire chief driving an ambulance came upon a group of cyclists and ordered them to ride single file. One of the cyclists responded "Go **** yourself." The chief threatened to take further action, to which the cyclist allegedly responded that he should, "Shove his radio up his ******* ***." The chief then alerted a police officer who cited the cyclist for disorderly conduct, and she was convicted at trial.

However, the 6th District Court of Appeals overturned the cyclist's conviction because even though she swore at the fire chief and upset him, her words did not amount to "fighting words" and were protected by the First Amendment (Amendment I). Cyclists can ride two abreast in Ohio.

Obviously, I support this correct result. But this is an example of where the cyclist may have opted to either ignore the unlawful command from the fire chief, or simply respond more calmly. A cyclist's reaction oftentimes determines the outcome of an encounter with authorities and other road users. In this case, the cyclist was rightfully able to get her conviction overturned on appeal, but she had to go through hell to get it.

*State v. Tudor, 118 N.E.3d 297 (Ohio Ct. App. 2019)*[106]

Case type: TRAFFIC OFFENSES—CYCLIST

At around 5:00 p.m. in August, a cyclist was riding his bike eastbound on Main Street in Ravenna's downtown commercial district. According to the police, this cyclist was riding ". . . in the center of the lane, holding a McDonald's cup in his left hand, and flapping or waving his right hand." The cyclist was charged with Reckless Operation of his bicycle, Obstructing Official Business and not Driving in Marked Lanes, all misdemeanor charges. The prosecutor did not pursue the Obstructing Official Business charge, but the municipal judge found the cyclist guilty of Reckless Operation. The cyclist appealed his conviction, but in a 2-1 decision, the 11th District Appellate Court of Portage County affirmed the lower court and upheld his conviction of Reckless Operation.

The Court reasoned that riding his bicycle with no hands while holding a cup, on a commercial street, compromised this cyclist's ability to steer and brake the bicycle, constituting a willful and wanton disregard for the safety of others. The cyclist argued that he was able to maintain control of his bicycle and that no injury had occurred, but this argument failed to convince the majority of the judges.

The dissenting judge said that the evidence showed the cyclist had control of his bicycle, and since there were parked motor vehicles off to his right, the cyclist had every reason to ride closer to the center of the lane. Even though this cyclist may have been an inconvenience to motorists behind him, he posed no threat to the safety of any person or property.

**This is an interesting case for a few reasons.** The dissent correctly pointed out that there were motor vehicles parked to the cyclist's right and riding closer to the center of the lane was practicable to avoid being "doored" by someone exiting a motor vehicle. However, this was not the majority opinion and illustrates the uncertainty that can occur when bike cases go before a court. I've seen many cyclists who were in complete control while riding with no hands (although I'm not one of them, *kudos* to anyone who is) and drinking from a water bottle or fishing around for an energy bar in their back pocket. In this case, the aggravating circumstances of having a cup in one hand and waving the other while riding in a commercial district pushed the Court over the edge to convict this cyclist, but it could have gone the other way.

However, if the actions of this cyclist here were sufficient to establish Reckless Operation, it stands to reason that a motorist driving while distracted is more of a threat, and the police and courts should consider distracted driving to be Reckless Operation under any interpretation of this case.

### *Ohio v. Copley* (Ohio, 2010)[107]

### Case type: CRIMINAL OFFENSE—MOTORIST

A motorist driving a van with three other occupants came upon a cyclist riding to work and through a loud speaker allegedly "complimented" the cyclist with, "Nice bike, ******" and "I'm going to get you off the road" while they were stopped at a red light. Still near each other a few blocks down the road at another red light, the cyclist allegedly responded by knocking on the side mirror of the van and asking, "What's the deal?" Both parties then proceeded through the light with the motorist allegedly sideswiping the cyclist and causing him slight injury.

At the trial level, a Cuyahoga County jury found the motorist guilty of felonious assault, which is defined as "**knowingly** causing physical harm by means of a deadly weapon." In this case, it was the van! However, on appeal of his conviction the 8th District Cuyahoga County Court of Appeals reversed, finding the evidence was insufficient to establish that the motorist "knowingly" attempted to cause the cyclist physical harm. The cyclist was sideswiped, not hit directly, and the Appeals Court noted the cyclist never fell off his bike. As obvious as it may be to some that sideswiping a person on a bike with a van is clearly dangerous, this Court determined that regardless of his purpose, the motorist's conduct failed to rise to the level of "knowingly" hurting the cyclist. The motorist's attorney successfully argued the driver didn't know sideswiping a cyclist would "probably" injure him.

This 2:1 decision again demonstrates that criminal conduct is fact driven and is another example of a decision that could have gone either way and actually resulted in a felony conviction for the motorist that was overturned on appeal. Motorists should know that when they intentionally hit a cyclist, even "gently," they can be charged (and possibly convicted) of felonious assault; a conviction that can include prison time. The other valuable lesson here as a cyclist is to try to avoid escalating a confrontation like this, although this abuse was hard to ignore. The better tactic may be just to stop and call the police if you are threatened.

*Cummings v. Lyles, 27 N.E.3d 985 (Ohio Ct. App. 2015)*[108]

## Case type: INSURANCE COVERAGE —INTENTIONAL ACTS

The 8th District Cuyahoga County Court of Appeals held that a motorist, who pled guilty to intentionally driving into and injuring a cyclist whom he believed had stolen his son's bike,

**was not covered** by the motorist's auto liability policy. Ohio law prohibits liability insurance from covering damages caused by intentional acts, since liability insurance does not exist to shield a person from intentional wrongdoing.

This case illustrates a dangerous potential obstacle to *civil* (non-criminal) justice for a cyclist intentionally hit by a motorist. A motorist who **intentionally** injures someone will have no applicable liability insurance coverage available to compensate that person for their injuries. This leaves the cyclist to try to recover against the motorist's personal assets, which may be few or nonexistent.

*Passwaters v. Knaur, 2006-Ohio-1518 (Ct. App.)*[109]

Case type: WRONGFUL DEATH OF A CYCLIST

A motorist was trying to pass another motor vehicle which was following closely behind two adolescents riding their bikes. As he attempted the maneuver, the motorist allegedly ran out of space as he approached a no passing zone while still positioned on the wrong side of the road. He beeped his horn, presumably to get the cyclists to move out of his way or to make room in the lane to accommodate his vehicle. One of the adolescent cyclists allegedly made a sharp left movement in front of the defendant and was tragically killed. The cyclist's family brought a wrongful death negligence suit against the motorist, but the jury found the motorist wasn't negligent and this outcome was affirmed on appeal.

It's hard to know exactly what the cyclist intended to do when he moved left, but it is unlikely he intended to put himself in danger. It seems far more likely that he was trying to avoid the source of the horn and misjudged where the sound was coming from. If a motorist sounds their horn—even with good intention—it can startle cyclists, and they might not know how to react. Please remember, cyclists, if someone in a motor vehicle sounds their horn while passing you on your bike, you want to try to stay to the right. If that's unsafe or not practical, hold your line and try to remain as predictable as possible.

*Deutsch v. Birk, 937 N.E.2d 638 (Ohio Ct. App. 2010)*[110]

Case type: MULTI-USE TRAIL—LIABILITY

An experienced cyclist riding on the multi-use Little Miami Bike Trail was severely injured when a young girl pushed her bicycle across the trail and into the path of the cyclist. The injured cyclist brought a negligence civil suit against the child to recover damages for his injuries. The Ohio 12th District Court of Appeals ruled that the child owed no duty to the injured cyclist because both were engaged in a recreational activity and "assumed the risks" inherent to the activity. Unless the child had acted in a legally reckless or willful manner, there would be no civil liability. The Court refused to apply the traffic laws applicable to bikes ridden on the road, reasoning that this was a multi-use trail including walking, jogging, skateboarding, rollerblading and horseback riding, and the laws the injured cyclist invoked were applicable only to bicycles operated on the road, or "on paths set aside for the exclusive use of bicycles."

While I do not agree with this decision that riding your bike on an all purpose trail is akin to playing football or baseball where one assumes the risk of the game, this is still a prime example of why cyclists who ride at higher speeds rightly have the option of riding on the road. The unpredictability and potential nonliability of other trail users, coupled with the speed differential between various trail users, offers strong justification for Ohio law providing cyclists with an absolute right to ride on the road if they so choose. This is not to say that you should refrain from riding on multi-use paths, but it is important to understand the risks of doing so and to tailor your riding and expectations appropriately.

*Crabtree v. Cook, 964 N.E.2d 473 (Ohio Ct. App. 2011)*[111]

Case type: POLITICAL SUBDIVISION LIABILITY—
ROAD CONDITIONS

In Columbus, two cyclists were riding beneath an underpass on a road that was littered with potholes and other road hazards. To avoid the hazards, one of the cyclists had to ride toward the center of the lane and he was hit from behind by a speeding motorist, rendering him a quadriplegic. At the trial level, in addition to suing this motorist, the cyclist sued the City of Columbus for "negligent failure to keep public roads in repair (or) other negligent failure to remove obstructions from public roads," as required by State statute. The City raised the defense of Governmental Immunity, a legal doctrine that acts as a shield from liability for municipalities, and also claimed that the potholes the cyclist was avoiding were merely a "nuisance" and not an "obstruction." The Trial Court agreed with the city and dismissed the suit.

The 10th District Court of Appeals of Franklin County reversed the Trial Court's decision and held that the City of Columbus was not immune from liability because an exception to the immunity shield exists when a political subdivision negligently fails to keep roads in repair or fails to remove "obstructions" from the public roads. Unlike the Trial Court, the Court of Appeals found that potholes are not just a nuisance for cyclists and under some circumstances they may also constitute an "obstruction" the City had a duty to remove.

Please note: this well-thought-out and just decision by the 10th District doesn't mean that all cyclists have a "clear road" to recover against political subdivisions i.e., cities, counties, and townships for road imperfections. Generally, cases against political subdivisions for road hazards are difficult and highly fact contingent. Even when an exception may exist, political subdivisions enjoy many other defenses not generally available to an individual or non-governmental entity. When in doubt, always seek the counsel of an experienced bike attorney.

### *Storc v. Day Drive* (Office Max) (Ohio, 2006)[112]

### Case type: PREMISE LIABILITY

A cyclist sued Office Max after his bike ran into a hole on the store's sidewalk at 10:30 at night. The trial court dismissed the case. In a split decision, the 8th District Cuyahoga County Court of Appeals affirmed that Office Max had no liability because the hole was an "open and obvious" danger, and that the attendant circumstance of it being dark did not excuse the cyclist of his failure to notice the hole until it was too late. Moreover, because the cyclist failed to submit evidence proving Office Max knew (or should have known) the hole existed, they had no duty to the cyclist.

This is an excellent example of how sidewalks can be fraught with dangers for cyclists, and how business or property owners are not responsible if the cyclist can't show that the owners created, or had knowledge of the defect, or if the defect was "open and obvious." Also! Please remember that it's often illegal to ride on the sidewalk in a business district.

## *Kane v. City of Dayton* (Ohio, 2018)[113]

## Case type: HOME RULE—OHIO REVISED CODE (ORC) v. LOCAL ORDINANCE

In Kane v. Dayton, Dayton's local ordinance relaxed Ohio law and only required bike lights to be on one hour **after** sunset. (Ohio law requires bike lights **at** sunset.) A cyclist was hit by a motor vehicle and injured within the one-hour period after sunset when he didn't have his lights on. Not having his lights on was legal under Dayton's ordinance, but it was illegal under the Ohio Revised Code.

The Court conducted a "home rule" analysis to determine that the Dayton ordinance must yield to state law because the ORC statue was a general law of Ohio designed to operate uniformly, prescribing conduct that applies to all citizens generally.

This case illustrates the importance of following state law concerning mandatory lights from sunset to sunrise, regardless of what you might see on your local books.

# 11

# CRASH
# STATISTICS
# & RANKINGS

# REPORT CARD:
# WHERE DOES OHIO RANK?

The League of American Bicyclists' Bicycle Friendly State Report Card has Ohio ranked at 18 out of 50.[114] Ranking is based on a comprehensive survey completed by state departments of transportation and state bicycling advocates. With a dual focus of celebrating successes and offering suggestions, letter grades are given for areas including **Legislation and Enforcement, Infrastructure & Funding,** and **Policies & Programs.** In the **Legislation & Enforcement** category, Ohio received an overall grade of C, but in the subcategory of distracted driving laws, it only earned a D+, illustrating the need for more comprehensive distracted driving laws and better use of photo enforcement.

These rankings and the associated data are sobering. The numbers represent human beings, any one of whom could be a colleague, a neighbor, a family member, or a friend.

When it comes to the likelihood of death or serious injury in a crash, speed matters! Studies show that when struck by a motor vehicle going 20 mph, an "average pedestrian" has only a seven percent chance of being killed. At 30 mph, the number jumps to 20 percent, and at 40 mph—a mere 10 mph higher—the likelihood of death leaps to around **80 percent**! The degree of vulnerability for cyclists is essentially the same as that of pedestrians, which makes sense; it's still flesh and bone against steel.

# BIKE CRASHES IN OHIO

In 2018, 124 cyclists across Ohio suffered serious injuries—a decrease from 174 the previous year, so that is an improvement—but it isn't all good news. 22 cyclists sadly lost their lives in 2018—an increase from 19 deaths in 2017, and a reminder that we must always remain vigilant both when we ride and drive.

# BIKE CRASHES IN CLEVELAND

Attention, Cleveland-area drivers: stats for Cleveland traffic safety are in, and at the time of writing they don't look good. QuoteWizard (an insurance aggregator that helps people compare policies) published a "2019 worst driving cities in America" list based on insurance analysis for the nation's largest 75 cities.[115] Factors included citations, speeding tickets, DUIs, and crashes. Cleveland ranked number seven in the top worst cities in which to drive, a dubious honor. Thankfully, Cleveland officials are taking note and aggressively moving forward with the upcoming "Vision Zero" legislation, which seeks to reduce to zero all deaths and serious injuries on our roads.

A disproportionate amount of bike crashes in Cleveland are happening on roads with speeds marked at 25 mph and higher, resulting in both injury and death. Beyond speed, poor visibility is a factor, which can be exacerbated by wintery conditions and inadequate street lighting.

Bike Cleveland shares information on its website about Cleveland's High Injury Network (identifying areas of particular danger), including rates of Fatal and Serious Injury on Cleveland's roads and where the "High Crash Hot Spots" are located.[116]

# BIKE CRASHES ACROSS THE U.S.

In October 2019, the U.S. Department of Transportation's National Highway Traffic Safety Administration (NHTSA) released fatal traffic crash data for calendar year 2018. According to the data, which was collected from all 50 states and the District of Columbia, in 2018 "pedalcyclist" deaths increased by 6.3 percent for a total of 859—the highest number of pedalcyclist fatalities since 1990![117] It's true that in 2017 pedalcyclist deaths had decreased by 8.1 percent—but 783 cyclists still lost their lives that year, which is far too many because in the words of U.S. Transportation Secretary Elaine L. Chao, ". . . nearly all crashes are preventable."[118]

# 12

# E-BIKES & OHIO LAW

**M**ore and more, "pedal powered" or "muscle bikes"— the kind we grew up with—are competing with another type of bike—the electric bike, or e-bike. E-bikes are the fastest-growing segment of the bike market in the United States. As of September 2018, one million e-bikes had been sold in the U.S. The cost—ranging from around $1,500 for a basic model to $10,000+ for a luxury ride—clearly isn't scaring away consumers!

Bike shops in the Greater Cleveland area and beyond stock e-bikes and road bikes including **but not limited to**: Spin Bike Shop,[119] new kid on the block Gear Up Velo,[120] Beat Cycles, Century Cycles, Blazing Saddle Cycle, Eddy's Bike Shop, Joy Machines Bike Shop, All-Around Cyclery, Cycle Sport and Fitness, Bike Authority, The Broadway Cyclery, Solon Bicycle, Cain Park Bicycle, Bicycle Boulevard, Bicycle Bill's (Vermilion) and Electric Pete's E-bikes (Akron). As e-bikes become more popular this list will only grow, and before long we might even start seeing used e-bikes work their way into the Ohio City Bicycle Co-op's fleet of used bikes for sale. Related, and recommended by the Heights Bicycle Coalition is Cleveland's Two One Fix Bicycle offering on-site and pick-up/drop-off bicycle maintenance and repair.

## WHAT IS AN E-BIKE?

E-bikes are low-speed bicycles equipped with electric motors that run on lithium-ion batteries. Battery, controller and motor are fully incorporated into the bike's componentry. E-bikes handle similarly to a regular bike, but they weigh more due to the motor and battery. They can still be pedaled if the battery runs out, and some classes of e-bikes are equipped with a throttle controlled by hand and don't require pedaling, while others provide an optional power boost when you turn the pedals, helping you to achieve a higher speed with less effort than you could achieve only using muscle power.

## E-BIKE BENEFITS

Moving at speeds like those of regular bicycles, e-bikes allow riders to climb hills with less effort and to extend trip lengths. These factors can encourage riders to bike more frequently, increasing the frequency of bikes on the road and normalizing their presence. E-bikes also offer a new recreation option for people with physical limitations that might prevent them from enjoying traditional bikes. With additional benefits of being emission-free and low impact with relatively silent operation, e-bikes are here to stay. They may be more expensive than traditional bikes, but they're still cost-effective in comparison to motor vehicles.[121]

## E-BIKE LEGISLATION BY STATE

Since 2015 there's been considerable statewide legislative action regarding e-bikes. Some of this action focused on revising older state laws that formerly classified e-bikes as mopeds or scooters, and addressing some of the burdensome licensure, registration or equipment requirements that existed. Instead, they adopted a three-tiered e-bike classification system based on speed capabilities and method of propulsion. At the time of writing, 33 states **including Ohio** plus the District of Columbia have an **electric bicycle definition** and laws governing their operation. In states that have not yet updated their laws, e-bikes aren't specifically defined and may be classified in the moped or motorized bicycle group.[122] If you're reading this and you don't live in Ohio, check your state's law.

## OHIO'S E-BIKE LAW

**Ohio** became the 11th state with an industry-supported e-bike law. Ohio House Bill 250 went into effect in March 2019, addressing requirements for electric bicycle use in Ohio and explicitly excluding e-bikes from the definition of motor vehicles.[123] Despite having a motor, e-bikes are classified as bicycles (and as such, vehicles) in Ohio. They have pedals and are usually muscle-assisted. **Like regular bikes, e-bikes don't require a license, registration or insurance.**

## OHIO'S THREE-TIERED E-BIKE CLASSIFICATION SYSTEM

Thirteen states **including Ohio** require that a label stating classification number, top assisted speed, and motor wattage be affixed to all e-bikes.[124]

Ohio law provides that:

- A **Class 1** e-bike is a bike with an electric motor which provides assistance only when the rider is pedaling, and ceases to assist once a speed of **20 mph** is reached[125]

- A **Class 2** e-bike is a bike with an electric motor which can propel the bike **without** pedaling, but will not provide assistance once a speed of **20 mph** is reached[126]

- A **Class 3** e-bike is similar to a Class 1 e-bike and provides assistance only when the rider is pedaling, and stops assisting once a speed of **28 mph** is reached[127]

Class 1 and Class 2 e-bikes are generally treated the same as traditional bicycles and are permitted on multi-use trails, but because of their higher speeds, Class 3 e-bikes capable of 28 mph are not generally allowed in such places and are reserved for the road. Additional regulations in Ohio include a bike helmet for anyone operating, or riding as a passenger, on a Class 3 e-bike,[128] and one must be at least 16 to operate a Class 3 electric bicycle (a person under the age of 16 may still ride as a passenger if that Class 3 e-bike is designed to carry passengers.)[129]

## WHERE TO RIDE E-BIKES

Bike Cleveland has a comprehensive resource page—which you should check periodically—that covers the definitions and permissions for e-bikes.[130] Following is a reproduction of some of that information regarding where we can ride each type of e-bike at the time of writing:

- Per the Ohio Revised Code (ORC), Class 1 and Class 2 electric bicycles may ride on paths that are shared use, or exclusively set aside for bikes, unless prohibited by a resolution, ordinance, or rule passed by a controlling entity (like a city, township, or other authority such as the Cleveland Metroparks, which is a state agency and political subdivision of Ohio)[131]

- A Class 3 electric bicycle is generally confined to the road and is allowed on a shared use path or bike path **only if the path is adjacent to a highway**, or if a controlling authority specifically granted permission[132]

**All classes** of electric bicycle are prohibited from riding on trails meant for mountain bike riders, hikers, horseback riders or similar users, unless special permission from a controlling authority has been granted.[133]

**Riding in the Cleveland Metroparks:** At the time of writing, all classes of e-bikes can be used on the roadways throughout the Metroparks—but **not** on all its mountain bike, hiking, or equestrian trails. Class 1 and Class 2 e-bikes can be ridden on the paved multi-use trails in the Cleveland Metroparks, provided they are ridden safely and respectfully around other park visitors. Class 3 e-bikes are prohibited on the multi-use trails in the Cleveland Metroparks.

**Riding in the Cuyahoga Valley National Park (CVNP):** In accordance with Ohio law, all classes of e-bikes can be used on the roadways throughout the CVNP, but there are limits regarding trail usage. Class 1 and Class 2 e-bikes are allowed on all trails available to bikes **except East Rim Mountain Bike Trail**, but **Class 3 e-bikes are prohibited on park trails.** Furthermore, the current guidelines from the CVNP require e-bikes can only be used in "pedal assist" mode, not solely with the throttle.

When in doubt as to where you can legally ride, look for a sign or a park representative before rolling into uncertain territory. Better yet, research the location beforehand!

## ELECTRIC MOUNTAIN BIKES

Despite what you may be seeing in mountain biking magazines, at the time of writing all e-bike classes are **prohibited** from use of **mountain bike trails** in the Cleveland Metroparks, CVNP, and Summit Metroparks.

**Always** check your local trail rules for any changes.

# 13

# THE EVOLUTION OF MICRO-MOBILITY DEVICES

T he list of micro-mobility device options is growing rapidly, and important differences exist between them.

# ELECTRIC SCOOTERS WITH NO SEAT/RIDER STANDING

You've likely seen these downtown. They include those manufactured by **Bird**, **Lime**, and **Spin**, all of which are available in Cleveland as of October 2019. Lyft and Uber (with its Jump e-scooter) also got in the game in 2018, but as of this writing were not yet in Cleveland.[134] Ohio House Bill 295 will establish statewide requirements governing low-speed micro-mobility devices and bring them into conformity with many of the laws that govern bikes and other vehicles. HB 295 passed in the Ohio House on February 12, 2020 and at the time of writing is under consideration in the Ohio Senate.[135] Until this bill passes, scooters will continue to be regulated by local law which has been updated more expediently.

## CLEVELAND E-SCOOTERS

In April 2019, Cleveland City Council unanimously approved regulations governing the business of e-scooters,[136] making good on its promise after "Birdgate" (when a large quantity of Bird e-scooters landed in the Cleveland with no previous warning by their manufacturer) to officially allow e-scooters in Cleveland.[137]

The approved regulations were part of Cleveland's 2019 electric scooter pilot project that set up targeted areas of the city including University Circle, the Euclid Corridor, downtown Cleveland, and Ohio City, to gauge scooter popularity and success.

Some of these new regulations include:

- Must be at least 18

- Cannot operate e-scooters over 12 mph[138]

- Must not ride on streets that have a 35 mph or higher speed limit[139]

- Must park e-scooters on sidewalks in a way that doesn't interfere with the flow of pedestrians[140]

- Must park e-scooters in an upright position[141]

- Must stay off sidewalks in business districts

The good news, beyond having another transportation choice, is the fee that vendors pay for each e-scooter rental will be used in part by the City to improve bike infrastructure.

During the pilot program, e-scooters were allowed to operate between 7 a.m. to 7 p.m. GPS technology and on-board controls prevent the scooter from operating outside designated areas or at unauthorized times. If you attempt to move a scooter illegitimately, an alarm will sound. Anyone wishing to use one must have an account with the company along with an app on their smartphone.

Dockless e-scooters and e-bikes are bound by all traffic rules applicable to bicycles. These devices can be ridden on roadways and in bike lanes, and riders should operate them as they would traditional bikes—keeping with the flow of road traffic, riding to the right, and staying off sidewalks in business districts or other areas with pedestrians. These e-scooters have built-in safety equipment like reflectors and lights. A free helmet upon request is a requirement of vendors with permits, but the reality is people generally forgo this. Use of Ohio's mandated hand signals outlined in Chapter Two of this book applies to these "mobility devices" as well, and only one rider at a time is permitted on them.

**Motorists** driving in the vicinity of a micro-mobility device must:

- Allow at least 3 feet between their vehicle and an e-bike or e-scooter rider

- Change lanes to pass a rider if insufficient room within the lane exists; remember, a double yellow line may be crossed if the scooter is moving at less than half the posted speed, the overtaking vehicle doesn't exceed the speed limit, and there is a sufficient sight line

- Be sure there's a safe amount of room before merging back in front of the rider, once motorist has passed them

Barring any of those circumstances, follow behind the rider at a safe distance until it's possible to safely pass them. E-scooters (and e-bikes) in Cleveland have the right of way in a bike lane and motorists must not impede their movement.

# WHEELS–SIMILAR, YET DISTINCT

"Wheels" arrived on Cleveland's micro-mobility scene after the scooters.[142] Wheels look a little like mopeds, are battery-operated, pedal-free, and allow the rider to either sit **or** stand. **Riders must be at least 18 years old and have a valid driver's license to use them.** Although the manufacturer refers to the units as "electric, shared bicycles", they run exclusively on battery power and don't really fit the description of a bicycle. They're defined as "Mobility Devices"[143] in Cleveland because they don't have operable pedals and don't meet the legal definition of any class of e-bike. However, because they are faster than the scooters, they tend to move similarly to bicycles, and the City of Cleveland elected to include them alongside shared dockless bikes and e-bikes in their permitting scheme. They can go up to 20 mph and can be ridden in Cleveland 24/7, although the company does take them offline during inclement weather in order to ensure rider safety.[144]

# 14

# THE RISE OF AUTONOMOUS VEHICLES (AVS)

A utomated Driving System (ADS) development has been going on for nearly a century, beginning with experiments in the 1920s, trials in the 1950s, and the first semi-automated car developed by Japanese engineers in 1977. The U.S. and Germany introduced the first autonomous (self-driving) vehicles in the 1980s.[145]

# LONG-DISTANCE AV TEST DRIVES

In 1995, the U.S. saw the inaugural long-distance test of a self-driving car. Dubbed "No Hands Across America", the vehicle was a Pontiac Transport minivan salvaged by a Delco engineering manager, and upgraded and test-driven by a research scientist and a then-Ph.D. student from the Carnegie Mellon University Robotics Institute.[146] "No Hands" traveled at an average speed of 63.8 mph with 98% of it—2,797 miles—completed autonomously.[147] Twenty years later in 2015, an Audi enhanced with Delphi technology went on a journey of over 3,400 miles through 15 states, with 99% of the trip made in self-driving mode.

Despite these successes, safety challenges exist on both the technical and the human sides of things. The vehicles must be capable of detecting—with the greatest of accuracy—humans and other vehicles (including bikes!) as well as the road. And humans must be able to clearly discern what an autonomous vehicle is going to do, which may be difficult without the benefit of traditional communication methods like hand signals and eye contact.

# LEGAL ISSUES SURROUNDING AVS

Liability concerning AVs is **a new and complex legal issue**. If a crash involves a vehicle utilizing software directed by Artificial Intelligence (AI) to drive itself, who's to blame? The vehicle manufacturer, the designer of the software/related technologies controlling the vehicle, the person riding in it, or the other motorist? At the time of writing, there's still no federal legislation regulating AVs due to the failed passage of the American Vision for Safer Transportation Through Advancement of Revolutionary Technologies (AV START) Act in the U.S. Senate in late 2018.[148] In the meantime, states are developing their own autonomous vehicle regulations, yet experts in the AV field fear regulatory uncertainty caused by different rules from state to state could stifle advancement. As of February 18, 2020, 29 states and the District of Columbia had enacted AV legislation, and 11 more states—**including Ohio**—have executive orders linked to AVs.[149]

# AV TESTING & ODOT'S DRIVEOHIO

In 2018, then-Gov. John Kasich signed an executive order for AV testing by way of DriveOhio. This new division of ODOT allows companies to test AVs once they've registered with the agency, and provided they have backup motorists in the vehicles ready to take over. Cities in Ohio including Dublin, Athens, Marysville, and Columbus have agreements with DriveOhio for testing AVs on their city streets, and there's a 35-mile-long section of U.S. Route 33 that Ohio has designated a "Smart Mobility Corridor" for the deployment of AVs.[150]

Ohio is also home to the $45 million SMART Testing center, a new addition to the Transportation Research Center (TRC) which has been testing vehicles for NHTSA since 1976.[151] Ohio partnered with The Ohio State University to provide the 540-acre SMART Center with a control center, a multi-lane road complete with an intersection and traffic signals, and an "indoor highway track" that can simulate a variety of weather conditions, including snow and ice, any time of year. However, the most impressive part of the SMART Center is its "urban network" simulating three city blocks. Autonomous vehicle technology can be tested in an area that includes intersections and traffic circles, and in situations with a "cyclist"—via "Kevin", an adult-sized test dummy on a bike, and a "pedestrian"—via a child-sized dummy called "Darek." Dog and deer dummies are also available.

# NATIONAL EFFORTS REGARDING AVS AND SAFETY

National bike organization, League of American Bicyclists believes that although AVs will eventually greatly reduce traffic injuries and fatalities, they also need to meet basic safety standards before being allowed in large numbers on our streets.[152] The League has called for a "vision test" that measures an AV's ability to recognize and respond to vulnerable road users including bicyclists and pedestrians, not just motor vehicles.

According to findings of the League, more and more vehicles with automatic emergency braking (AEB) systems are being allowed out on our roadways even though NHTSA hasn't been running all the appropriate tests regarding Bicyclist Detection Capability. Although NHTSA announced in 2019 its plans for "proposal of major upgrades" to the New Car Assessment Program (NCAP) at some point in 2020,[153] at the time of writing, there's no information on the Dummy Management Team page[154] of NHTSA's website indicating a plan for developing a test mannequin for bicyclist safety.

Findings of a study by the American Automobile Association (AAA)[155] also show the need for better pedestrian-detection technology testing. The testing of four car models—including sedans from Honda, Chevrolet, Tesla and Toyota—found that the technology failed in some of the most dangerous situations and frequently at night. Worse, when the cars were going just 20 mph, **every** tested vehicle had trouble with **every** single test. One simulation, recreating a child going between parked vehicles and out onto the road, resulted in the child being hit **nearly 90 percent of the time**. And once a test car was going at least 30 miles per hour and/or it was after dark, **the technology didn't work at all**! Sensors including radar and cameras are supposed to alert a driver of a motor vehicle when there's one or more people in its path and the vehicle should apply the brakes when the motorist's reactions aren't fast enough. Sounds great in theory, and auto manufacturers are boasting of these new systems in their advertising, yet with AAA reporting such abysmal test results it's scary to think of motorists over-relying on these features and being even **less** careful.

# 15

# WORKING ON BIKE SAFETY

A s an attorney, a significant part of my job includes assessing risk, and I have frequent contact with people who find themselves in a bad situation. I'm conscious that this book discusses crashes and the dangers of cycling, but I'm also aware that there are many people throughout the nation working on bike safety, and things appear to be heading in the right direction. The following is a sample of some of the initiatives being pursued at the federal, state, and local levels.

# FEDERAL ACTION (FAST ACT AND TAP)

The **Transportation Alternatives Program (TAP)** has historically been a critical funding source for bicycle infrastructure. The **FAST Act** "eliminates the MAP-21 Transportation Alternatives Program (TAP) and replaces it with a set-aside of Surface Transportation Block Grant (STBG) program funding for transportation alternatives (TA). These set-aside funds include all projects and activities that were previously eligible under the old TAP, encompassing a variety of smaller-scale transportation projects such as pedestrian and bicycle facilities, recreational trails, safe routes to school projects, community improvements such as historic preservation and vegetation management, and environmental mitigation related to stormwater and habitat connectivity."[156]

# FEDERAL HR 1507: THE BICYCLE COMMUTER ACT OF 2019

Cyclists commuting to work from 2009 to 2017 were able to receive a small tax benefit for doing so. In 2018, this bike commuter benefit, minimal though it was, got suspended via a provision in the federal Tax Cut and Jobs Act of 2018.

This didn't sit well with three bipartisan lawmakers, Reps. Ayanna Pressley of Massachusetts, Earl Blumenauer of Oregon, and Verne Buchanan of Florida. So, on March 5, 2019 they introduced Federal HR 1507: the "Bicycle Commuter Act of 2019". Not merely as a reinstatement of the previous plan with its low, flat rate, this new program would offer a bicycle benefit of 20% of the current $265 monthly deduction for motorists and public transport commuters, roughly $53 per month, allowing the benefit for bikes to rise along with that of other means of transportation. It would provide "a full pre-tax deduction to help cover cyclists' commuting costs" including "repairs, tune-ups…a bike share membership" or even the cost of "a cheap bike over time."[157]

Unfortunately, as of March 5, 2019, no further action had been taken on HR 1507, but advocates have not given up hope of it passing.[158]

# AMERICAN TRANSPORTATION INFRASTRUCTURE ACT (ATIA)

On July 30, 2019 a U.S. Senate committee passed America's Transportation Infrastructure Act (ATIA, S. 2302.)[159] In the early stages yet holding great promise, ATIA would reauthorize federal transportation policy, the current authorization of which expires September 2020, and give a huge monetary boost to bike infrastructure projects. The bill would ease the way for state and local planners to proceed toward goals of improved safety and accessibility for all riders. PeopleForBikes believes the ATIA would help bring bike infrastructure more fully into the 21st century, making the safety of pedestrians and cyclists a priority while recognizing the enormous benefits to the environment.[160]

# PROPOSED STATE AND LOCAL ACTION: OHIO HOUSE BILL 97

On February 21, 2019, the Ohio House of Representatives introduced House Bill 97,[161] which would require anyone operating or riding as a passenger on a bicycle to wear a helmet if they are not at least 18 years old. HB 97's secondary goal is the establishment of the Bicycle Safety Fund. The Bill was referred to the Transportation and Public Safety Committee in early March 2019 and had its first hearing on March 12, 2019. At the time of writing, this is the latest information on HB 97.

## OHIO HOUSE BILL 468

On January 14, 2020—after communicating with constituent Sharon Montgomery, whose husband John was tragically killed when they were in a crash caused by a distracted motorist[162]— State Rep. Mary Lightbody (D-Westerville) introduced House Bill 468 for safer roads in Ohio.[163] This legislation is one of the first steps toward making driving a motor vehicle while using a handheld electronic device a **primary offense** for all Ohioans.

# OHIO SENATE BILL 285

In related news, Ms. Montgomery testified on May 27, 2020 in support of Ohio Senate Bill 285 which would make distracted driving a primary offense, revising laws related to both distracted driving and, as addressed by Ohio House Bill 468, the use of electronic handheld devices while driving. As of this writing, no further committee action had been taken.

# OHIO HOUSE BILL 710

Introduced on June 25, 2020, Ohio House Bill 710 seeks to amend current sections of the Ohio Revised Code and to "prohibit police officers from engaging in biased policing and other status-based profiling and to require the attorney general's office to establish rules regarding such police practices."[164] Particularly notable for cyclists are ORC 109.805, which addresses the need to eradicate racial profiling, and ORC 2933.85, which would make it illegal for police officers to target people, including those on bicycles.

# OHIO SENATE BILL 73

In February 2020, the Ohio Senate unanimously passed Senate Bill 73—broadening the legal requirements to ensure pedestrian safety at sidewalks and intersections—and in May 2020 it was introduced to the House and referred to committee.[165] This Bill has support and I fully expect it to pass, adding more protection for pedestrians around places with higher crash rates.

# SAFE ROUTES TO SCHOOLS

With the greater safety and health of Cleveland's children in grades K-8 in mind, the July 2015 planning meeting for the Ohio Safe Routes to School (SRTS) Program included representatives from ODOT, the City of Cleveland, area police departments, medical facilities and foundations, and Bike Cleveland. Established by the U.S. Department of Transportation (U.S. DOT), the Safe Routes to School program is designed to make safer the routes children take to and from school, thus reducing the number of motor vehicles dropping off and picking up kids and helping parents be more comfortable with their kids walking and biking to school. This has the added benefit of building physical activity into the everyday movements of kids in our community, which will only help them live longer, healthier lives. Safe Routes to School uses the "five Es" to make routes to school safer:

- **Education**—Teaching students how to walk and ride to school safely

- **Encouragement**—Using activities and programs to make walking and biking fun and safe

- **Engineering**—Improving sidewalks and roads

- **Enforcement**—Working with police, crossing guards, and community members to make sure that laws are being followed

- **Evaluation**—Checking that the actions taken are making a difference

This comprehensive approach does far more than most programs and has achieved such unorthodox successes as adding bicycle skills and education classes to the 3$^{rd}$ grade

P.E. The Cleveland Metropolitan School District continues this program locally with the support of NOACA, the City of Cleveland, ODOT, and Bike Cleveland.[166]

Calley Mersmann, Cleveland's current Bicycle and Pedestrian Coordinator at the time of writing, was there from the beginning as the Cleveland Metropolitan School District Safe Routes to School Coordinator before taking on her new role as the Bicycle and Pedestrian Coordinator and playing a pivotal role in the advancement of Vison Zero.

## ODOT'S WALK.BIKE.OHIO

The Ohio Department of Transportation (ODOT) is developing the State's first-ever walking and biking plan, Walk.Bike.Ohio, to act as a guide for future transportation policies and allocation of funding for programs and infrastructure. The plan utilizes "Demand Analysis"—a process that estimates the cumulative demand for active transportation by quantifying factors that lead to walking and biking, and provides a composite score for equally weighted variables such as population density, employment centers, schools and universities, parks, and poverty metrics. The plan is expected to be complete by December 2020,[167] and a final Pedestrian Safety Analysis report including recommendations for new policies and steps for achievement was submitted in February 2020 to the Division of Planning/Office of Statewide Planning.

## CUYAHOGA GREENWAYS

Known as "Cuyahoga Greenways" today, this effort began in 2014 as the "Trails Leadership Network" and consists of many stakeholders. Currently headed by perhaps the three most important regional entities when it comes to alternative transportation—Cuyahoga County Planning Commission, Cleveland Metroparks, and NOACA—Cuyahoga Greenways represents continued collaboration toward achieving a comprehensive and extensive system of trails, bikeways, and pedestrian routes across Cuyahoga County. The goal is to ultimately build and connect a network of trails, paths, and on-street facilities so people throughout the county can access safe and inviting recreational opportunities and active transportation.

Much of this network already exists but isn't connected, so the focus is on identifying the missing links that make it difficult to get around by bike or on foot. This is a visionary project with a long lifespan and if achieved, it will bring long lasting benefits to the region as people increasingly choose where they live based on these kinds of amenities. People don't want to drive. They want to bike, and this will help them do it.

This project also has the support of the Cleveland Planning Commission and according to its Director, (as well as Co-Chair of the Vision Zero Design and Engineering Subcommittee) Freddy L. Collier Jr., "There is enthusiasm to make sure that all residents in all of our cities throughout the county have an opportunity to connect."[168]

# COMPLETE AND GREEN STREETS INITIATIVE (CGS)

"Complete Streets" is a term used in urban planning, transportation advocacy, and roadway and traffic engineering to mean streets that do more than merely funnel motor vehicles through; Complete Streets focuses on improved safety, health, economic and environmental outcomes. Complete Streets places significant emphasis on safe access for **all** users—including pedestrians, cyclists, people making deliveries, and those riding public transportation.

Varying design elements come into play in the makeup of Complete Streets depending on the need, but can include median crossing islands, curb extensions, the elimination of free-flow right-turn lanes, angled parking that faces outward, and curb corner radii that is shorter (all of which help to calm traffic), and yes, specific accommodations for bikes like protected/dedicated lanes.

The City of Cleveland has had Complete and Green Streets legislation on its books since 2012, and it calls for the city to consider a wide array of issues whenever a road is repaved. Critics contend that this was applied inconsistently—with Cleveland not always living up to its own legislation—and have been calling for better oversight and more robust CGS legislation. These calls have been answered with Cleveland updating its CGS ordinance as part of its more comprehensive work on Vision Zero, and safety advocates hope that this new iteration will bring more uniform change in a way that the 2012 legislation was unable to do.[169]

# GROWTH IN OHIO BICYCLE INFRASTRUCTURE, INCLUDING PROTECTED BIKE LANES

Good things are happening in Cleveland! Bike lane mileage is up, and Cleveland is even beginning to install protected bike lanes in some areas with plans for more! The Northeast Ohio

Areawide Coordinating Agency (NOACA)[170] has allocated funds for upcoming projects and recently helped create the City's first protected bike lane. And, there is more to come!

In 2020, a $8.3 million construction project will begin on The Midway—Cleveland's Protected Bikeway Network's[171] first section—with a 2.5-mile route down the center of Superior Avenue and running from Public Square to East 55th Street. The ultimate vision for the Midway is a "bicycle highway" system making the most of underutilized roads once used by streetcars and designed to carry a far greater motor vehicle load than is asked of them today. When complete, The Midway will extend for more than 50 miles in all directions throughout Cleveland. More construction is planned for 2022 utilizing NOACA's allocation of $6.1 million. Conceptually approved by the Cleveland City Planning Commission in 2015, the Lorain Avenue Cycle Track will be integrated into The Midway network, helping to better connect people to a historic shopping district and hopefully boost economic development. Bike Cleveland thinks that once these projects are completed, they will " . . . put Cleveland on the route to a network of **world-class** sustainable transportation infrastructure."

# VISION ZERO LEGISLATION AND CLEVELAND'S SIDE GUARD INITIATIVE

Beyond this, Cleveland officials are moving forward with the upcoming "Vision Zero" legislation, which seeks to reduce to zero all deaths and serious injuries on our roads. The City is taking pedestrian and bike crashes seriously and it is using data and intelligent planning principles to help reach this goal. Cleveland has even identified its high crash corridors and is actively seeking to address them through its Vision Zero and "Complete & Green Streets" legislation. Bike Cleveland collaborated with the Vision Zero Task Force Data and Evaluation Subcommittee to analyze serious injuries and fatalities caused by crashes and presents the data—including a high injury network map—on its website.[172]

Along with Truck Safety Attorney Andrew Young of Leizerman & Young LLP,[173] Ken is an original member of Cleveland's "Vision Zero Taskforce". Andy and Ken have continued focusing on lateral safety devices known as "side guards" which are installed on the sides of large commercial trucks between the front and rear wheels. In a commercial truck crash involving a cyclist or pedestrian, it's not the initial impact that typically kills or maims, but when the cyclist or pedestrian is pulled under the truck through the exposed area or gap on the side between the wheels, and then run over by the larger rear wheels in a horrible situation known as "underride."

The City of Cleveland and attorney Andy Young deserve credit for initiating the side guard program and meaningfully pursuing Vision Zero goals, with additional credit for recognizing the need to clarify and expand its Complete & Green Streets ordinances with input from Cleveland's Vision Zero Taskforce. The Cleveland Vision Zero Taskforce is comprised of five subcommittees and has experienced significant growth since its inception in early 2018. In the Bibliography is a link[174] to a document—provided by the extremely helpful Anne Tillie, Research and Policy Analyst for Cleveland City Council and member of the Data and Evaluation Subcommittee—noting all of those involved as of this writing, including numerous individuals in addition to the official subcommittees and their respective chairs. Cleveland's larger Vision Zero push is headed by Councilman Matt Zone (Chairman of the Safety Committee), and Darnell Brown (Chief Operating Officer, City of Cleveland).

# A FINAL NOTE FROM THE AUTHOR...

Ultimately, motorist education, awareness, and understanding concerning cyclist rights and their vulnerability on the road are some of the most important and effective ways to reduce the amount of crashes. Cyclists should know their rights **and** their responsibilities as well, but the onus should really be on motorists given the lopsided nature of vulnerability between cyclists and motorists. Practicing Vehicular Cycling can help to decrease friction and crashes when better infrastructure is lacking, but "Share the Road" cannot be mere verbiage; it must have teeth in the form of **legal consequences** for motorists failing to heed this adage. At the end of the day, we're dealing with life and limb out there. So remember, slow down, calm down, and remember that bikes are co-equal users of our roadways worthy of respect.

# LET'S ALL BE PART OF THE CONVERSATION!

# EPILOGUE

## IT'S REALLY
## WORTH IT!

# THE ENVIRONMENTAL IMPACT OF CYCLING (AIR AND WATER)

O ne of the reasons so many people choose to ride, and so many people and organizations are working to make it easier, is because of the massively positive impact more people on bikes has on our environment. And not just on the natural environment, but on the built environment and human systems we navigate every day. Given that transportation is the largest sector of carbon emissions in the U.S., the idea of "tackling climate change from the street up" by reducing motor vehicle emissions is gaining a lot of traction, and the fact is, we have known for decades how important bikes can be.[175]

We already know that the transportation sector is the biggest contributor of greenhouse gas emissions in the United States at over 28% of the country's total, and we know that around 80% of the carbon monoxide in our air comes from motor vehicles.[176] The impact on climate change is well documented and should not be ignored, and it needs to be understood how even a small switch from motor vehicles to bikes can make an enormous difference. For example, a 2008 study by Transportation Alternatives found that if 5% of New Yorkers commuting by private motor vehicle or taxi switched to bikes, it would prevent 150 million pounds of CO2 emissions getting pumped into the atmosphere every year. That's equivalent to the amount of carbon capture planting a forest 1.3 times the size of Manhattan would achieve.

But local air quality is another major issue that bikes can help to address. For example, according to the EPA, the Cleveland area has been in nonattainment territory for ground level ozone for eight of the last nine years. Ground level ozone causes respiratory and other cardiopulmonary problems, and you guessed it, motor vehicles deserve a large chunk of the blame because the nitrous oxide and other Volatile Organic Compounds (VOCs) motor vehicles produce create ozone. We have already seen how a reduction of motor vehicle miles improves air quality and in turn human health. For example, when motor vehicle travel restrictions reduced morning traffic by 23% during the 1996 Olympics in Atlanta, ozone concentrations decreased 28% and acute care visits for asthma decreased 41%.[177] A 2010 Wisconsin study showed that if 20% of people chose to use bikes for short trips (less than 5 miles) it would dramatically reduce the tonnage of $CO_2$ that gets pumped into the air each day, and the combined value of better air quality and reduced GHG emissions are estimated to save the state budget $90 million. There's nothing special about Wisconsin in this regard; this is something that can be done everywhere. With Covid-19 resulting in motor vehicle use decline and a bicycle boom, we have seen a worldwide drop in emissions!

Beyond air, people often don't realize the impact motor vehicles have on our water, and given our mostly flat topography (making it easier to ride around without hills) and location on the banks of Lake Erie, places like Cleveland stand to win big if we can get more people on bikes. As long as motor vehicles use oil, grease, rubber, coolants, and chemicals they will always deposit these on our roadways to be washed down the drain each and every time it rains. It has been shown that more bikes and less motor vehicles naturally reduce all of these things, but when you go a step further and start designing Complete and Green Streets for multimodal use and integrate smart design features like bioswales, planted medians, and using more permeable materials where possible, you can capture a lot of this pollution before it makes it to the lake, while making our streetscapes nicer, more inviting places.

# ECONOMIC IMPACT OF BIKES (SAVINGS, LAND USE, TOURISM)

Beyond the natural environment, there are real economic benefits to more bikes on the road and the associated infrastructure improvements that we are beginning to see with this new reality. Even if you don't ride, you want to live near to places where people do. It has been shown that proximity to quality bicycle infrastructure like protected bike lanes and trails increases property values. In fact, one study of homes near the Monon bike trail in Indianapolis revealed an 11% increase in the prices of the homes with the trail near them, and real estate agents frequently use bike lanes and similar infrastructure as selling points.[178] Famously, property values of homes adjacent to the Indianapolis Cultural Trail yielded a $1.01 billion increase in value.

Beyond this, bikes are good for tourism. In North Carolina, mountain bikers from elsewhere pump $30 million a year into the local economy,[179] and a study out of Arkansas showed that cycling generates $137 million annually in economic benefits to Northwest Arkansas which "validates cycling as a regional economic engine that supports local businesses, attracts tourists and builds healthier communities."[180] Closer to home, according to a user survey, 90,000 visitors spend $13 million on good and services related to the trails in Ohio's Miami Valley. It makes sense, because it has been shown that people on bikes spend more dollars on average than their motor vehicle-driving counterparts. So, if you see people riding around your business district, it's probably a good sign that things are healthy!

# THE LIVABILITY FACTOR IN LOCATION . . . AND, RELOCATION

When it comes to what makes a city or town "livable", ease of mobility and transportation choice are important factors. In a report by Livability.com[181] focusing on Millennials, "quality of life" is a major factor when deciding where to live. Forty percent of respondents cited "easy commutes, accessibility, walkability and bike friendliness" in their top influencers. One respondent who had been living in Chicago and experiencing little access to nature stated that "affordable housing, outdoor climbing and hiking, (and) bike friendly" were critical factors. In other words, any new location they'd consider would have to support a vibrant quality of life with plenty of time outdoors. So, if you're an elected official or a city planner/engineer concerned with population decline, continuing to develop better bike and pedestrian infrastructure, and demonstrating commitment to this generation by meeting their transportation preferences is necessary if you want your community to grow and thrive.

# BIKES ARE GOOD FOR YOUR HEALTH

So, bikes are good for the environment, good for our wallets, and good for where we live. It should be no surprise to learn that bikes are just straight up good for YOU! An exceptionally well-controlled study tracking 263,450 people over five years found that those who biked or walked to work had 41% lower risk of dying from all causes of death than those who drove or caught public transport.[182] The longer the distanced travelled, the greater the benefit. You might be thinking, "I exercise so this isn't for me," but it has also been shown that integrating biking into your everyday movements has powerful personal benefits, and even if you're active at other times, people who commute by motor vehicle are still more likely to gain more weight than their cycling counterparts.[183]

# THE BOTTOM LINE

The verdict is in. Bikes are good! Bikes are healthy and fun; bikes promote clean air and water; bikes make our cities less congested and safer; bikes save us money; and if we let them, bikes might just help us to save the world. While that is happening, and while you're actively participating in the solution, make sure you know your cycling rights and **make sure you cycle right!**

# BIBLIOGRAPHY

**C**ited websites and other sources current at time of writing.

As it becomes available, updates and other information regarding legislation, cycling laws, and more will be found at:

https://klfohio.com/cycling-rights-book/

1.  Cleveland Clinic/VeloSano, Home page. Accessed February 3, 2019. https://www.velosano.org/home

2.  Ohio to Erie Trail Fund, Home page. Accessed July 7, 2019. http://ohiotoerietrail.org/

3.  Wahoo Fitness, Bike Trainer page, accessed July 24, 2020. https://www.wahoofitness.com/devices/bike-trainers/view-all

4.  Zone, Matt. "In the Zone." Cleveland City Council. Published Spring 2018, accessed August 7, 2019. http://www.clevelandcitycouncil.org/ClevelandCityCouncil/media/CCCMedia/Publications/Ward%2015/zone_spring18-web.pdf

5.  Vision Zero Network, About page. Accessed February 5, 2019. https://visionzeronetwork.org/about/what-is-vision-zero/

6.  Bike Cleveland, Home page. Accessed February 5, 2019. https://www.bikecleveland.org/

7.  Ohio Bicycle Federation, Home page. Accessed February 5, 2019. http://www.ohiobike.org/

8.  VeloFemme-Litzler, Home page. Accessed February 5, 2019. http://velofemme.org/

9.  Team Spin/Litzler Automation, https://www.facebook.com/teamspinohio/ (Accessed February 5, 2019)

10. Cleveland Velodrome, Home page. Accessed February 5, 2019. http://clevelandvelodrome.org/

11. The League of American Bicyclists, Home page. Accessed February 5, 2019. https://www.bikeleague.org/

12. Bike Cleveland, Bikes and the Law page. Accessed February 5, 2019. https://www.bikecleveland.org/resources/bikes-and-the-law/

13. Francis Bacon. *Meditations Sacrae and Human Philosophy*, Whitefish, MT: Facsimile Reprint, Kessinger Publishing, LLC 2010

14. 45 Ohio Rev. Code. § 4511.07(A)(8) (2006), available at http://codes.ohio.gov/orc/4511.07

15. Ohio Department of Transportation's CYCLING SMARTER GUIDE: http://www.dot.state.oh.us/Divisions/Planning/SPR/bicycle/Documents/ODOTCyclingSmarterGuide.pdf

16. 45 Ohio Rev. Code. § 4501.01(A)(K) (2019), available at http://codes.ohio.gov/orc/4501.01

17. 45 Ohio Rev. Code. § 4511.01(A)(G) (2019), available at http://codes.ohio.gov/orc/4511.01

18. 45 Ohio Rev. Code. § 4511.52(A) (2019), available at http://codes.ohio.gov/orc/4511.52

19. Reid, Carlton. "Death of A 'Dinosaur:' Anti-Cycleway Campaigner John Forester Dies, Aged 90." *Forbes*, April 23, 2020. https://www.forbes.com/sites/carltonreid/2020/04/23/death-of-a-dinosaur-anti-cycleway-campaigner-john-forester-dies-aged-90/?fbclid=IwAR0EGVUs3tyvl3P30fa8cMqL9Zq2j0EiEIXbVV2wzxb7a_WREE_Xl8-uhbc36b42cd51cc3

20. John Forester. *Effective Cycling*, Cambridge, MA: 7th edition, MIT Press 2012

21. 45 Ohio Rev. Code. § 4511.051(A)(2) (2019), available at http://codes.ohio.gov/orc/4511.051

22. 45 Ohio Rev. Code. § 4511.07(A)(8) (2006), available at http://codes.ohio.gov/orc/4511.07

23. 45 Ohio Rev. Code. § 4511.01(YY) (2019), available at http://codes.ohio.gov/orc/4511.01

24. Bishop-Henchman, Joseph. "Gasoline Taxes and User Fees Pay for Only Half of State & Local Road Spending." Tax Foundation, January 3, 2014. https://taxfoundation.org/gasoline-taxes-and-user-fees-pay-only-half-state-local-road-spending/

25. Johnson, Amanda. "Ohio lawmakers contemplate increasing gas tax to fund road repairs." The Center Square, February 8, 2019. https://www.thecentersquare.com/ohio/ohio-lawmakers-contemplate-increasing-gas-tax-to-fund-road-repairs/article_6305d9e6-2b02-11e9-be3f-f72a50ab46f1.html

26. "Who Pays for Roads?" Frontier Group & U.S. PIRG Education Fund, Spring 2015. https://uspirg.org/sites/pirg/files/reports/Who%20Pays%20for%20Roads%20vUS.pdf

27. Ibid.

28. Carlton Reid. *Roads Were Not Built for Cars,* Washington DC: 2nd edition, Island Press 2015

29. 45 Ohio Rev. Code. § 4511.07(A)(8) (2006), available at http://codes.ohio.gov/orc/4511.07

30. 45 Ohio Rev. Code. § 4511.711(A) (2019), available at http://codes.ohio.gov/orc/4511.711

31. 45 Ohio Rev. Code. § 4511.55 (A)(C) (2019), available at http://codes.ohio.gov/orc/4511.55

32. 45 Ohio Rev. Code. § 4511.55(C) (2019), available at http://codes.ohio.gov/orc/4511.55

33. 45 Ohio Rev. Code. § 4511.31(B)(1)(2)(3) (2018), available at http://codes.ohio.gov/orc/4511.31

34. 45 Ohio Rev. Code. § 4511.55(B) (2019), available at http://codes.ohio.gov/orc/4511.55

35. 45 Ohio Rev. Code. § 4511.711(A) (2019), available at http://codes.ohio.gov/orc/4511.711

36. "Rules of the Road for Bicyclists." City of Columbus, Ohio. Accessed April 22, 2020. https://www.columbus.gov/ uploadedFiles/Columbus/Programs/Get_Active/Biking/ RulesOfTheRoad%20(1).pdf

37. Cincinnati, Ohio, Municipal Code of Ordinances Title V-Traffic Code, Chapter 506-Operation and Right of Way, § 506-5 (1972), available at https://library.municode.com/oh/ cincinnati/codes/code_of_ordinances?nodeId=TITVTRCO CH506OPRIWA_S506-5BIOPMI

38. "Bicycle Safety." National Highway Traffic Safety Administration (NHTSA). Accessed April 22, 2020. https:// www.nhtsa.gov/sites/nhtsa.dot.gov/files/811557.pdf

39. 45 Ohio Rev. Code. § 4511.711(A) (2019), available at http:// codes.ohio.gov/orc/4511.711

40. 45 Ohio Rev. Code. § 4511.441(A) (2018), available at http:// codes.ohio.gov/orc/4511.441

41. Cleveland, Ohio, Municipal Code, Part Four-Traffic Code, Title IX-Pedestrians, Bicycles and Motorcycles, Chapter 473-Bicycles, Motorcycles, Mobility Devices, § 473.09(c) (2019), available at https://codelibrary.amlegal.com/codes/ cleveland/latest/cleveland_oh/0-0-0-25132JD_473.09

42. 45 Ohio Rev. Code. § 4511.52(A) (2019), available at http:// codes.ohio.gov/orc/4511.52

43. 45 Ohio Rev. Code. § 4511.12(A) (2018), available at http:// codes.ohio.gov/orc/4511.12

44. 45 Ohio Rev. Code. § 4511.13(C)(1)(a)(b) (2013), available at http://codes.ohio.gov/orc/4511.13

45. 45 Ohio Rev. Code. § 4511.43(A) (2018), available at http:// codes.ohio.gov/orc/4511.43

46. Hilkevitch, Jon. "City says Dearborn bike signals keeping cyclists in line." *Chicago Tribune* (Chicago, Illinois), June 10, 2013. https://www.chicagotribune.com/autos/ct-xpm-2013-06- 10-ct-met-getting-around-0610-20130610-story.html

47. 45 Ohio Rev. Code. § 4511.40(A)(1)(2)(3)(B) (2019), available at http://codes.ohio.gov/orc/4511.40

48. 45 Ohio Rev. Code. § 4511.39(A) (2019), available at http://codes.ohio.gov/orc/4511.39

49. 45 Ohio Rev. Code. § 4511.56(A)(1)(2)(3)(B) (2019), available at http://codes.ohio.gov/orc/4511.56

50. 45 Ohio Rev. Code. § 4511.56(A)(2)(3) (2019), available at http://codes.ohio.gov/orc/4511.56

51. Bike Helmet Safety Institute, Bike Helmet Laws page. Accessed April 16, 2020. https://www.helmets.org/mandator.htm

52. Bicycle Helmet Safety Institute, Statistics page. Accessed March 17, 2019. https://helmets.org/stats.htmeffectiveness

53. MIPS, About page. Accessed August 29, 2019. http://www.mipscorp.com/om-mips/?lang=en

54. Lindsey, Joe. "Trek's WaveCel Helmet Technology Is Causing Controversy." *Outside,* April 2, 2019. https://www.outsideonline.com/2392896/trek-wavecel-helmet-controversy

55. Mayo Foundation for Medical Education and Research (MFMER), Post-concussion syndrome page. Accessed August 29, 2019. https://www.mayoclinic.org/diseases-conditions/post-concussion-syndrome/symptoms-causes/syc-20353352

56. 45 Ohio Rev. Code. § 4511.52(B)(D) (2019), available at http://codes.ohio.gov/orc/4511.52

57. 45 Ohio Rev. Code. § 4511.27(A)(1) (2019), available at http://codes.ohio.gov/orc/4511.27

58. Cleveland, Ohio, Municipal Code, Part Four-Traffic Code, Title Five-Vehicles, Chapter 431-Operation Generally, § 431.03(2)(b) (2019), available at https://www.amlegal.com/codes/client/cleveland_oh/

59. 45 Ohio Rev. Code. § 4511.132(A)(1)(2)(3) (2019), available at http://codes.ohio.gov/orc/4511.132

60. 45 Ohio Rev. Code. § 4511.36(A)(2) (2018), available at http://codes.ohio.gov/orc/4511.36

61. 45 Ohio Rev. Code. § 4511.39(A) (2019), available at http://codes.ohio.gov/orc/4511.39

62. 45 Ohio Rev. Code. § 4511.36(A)(1) (2018), available at http://codes.ohio.gov/orc/4511.36

63. "Bike Boxes." National Association of Transportation Officials (NACTO). Accessed June 3, 2019. https://nacto.org/publication/urban-bikeway-design-guide/intersection-treatments/bike-boxes/

64. "Urban Bikeway Design Guide." National Association of Transportation Officials (NACTO). Accessed June 3, 2019. https://nacto.org/publication/urban-bikeway-design-guide/

65. National Association of Transportation Officials (NACTO), "Don't Give Up at the Intersection: NACTO Releases Best Practices for Next-Generation Street Intersection Design," News release, (May 20, 2019). Accessed June 5, 2019. https://nacto.org/2019/05/20/dont-give-up-at-the-intersection/?utm_source=NACTO+Newsletter&utm_campaign=a965077874-EMAIL_CAMPAIGN_2019_04_22_04_58_COPY_01&utm_medium=email&utm_term=0_8f3492144e-a965077874-1204371949&mc_cid=a965077874&mc_eid=af74595ec0

66. "Don't Give Up at the Intersection." National Association of Transportation Officials (NACTO). Accessed June 6, 2019. https://nacto.org/publication/urban-bikeway-design-guide/dont-give-up-at-the-intersection/

67. Cleveland City Planning Commission, Bikeway Master Plan/Sharrows page. Accessed August 27, 2019. http://www.city.cleveland.oh.us/CityofCleveland/Home/Community/GettingAround

68. McEntee, Brian. "No, Really, What Are Sharrows Good For?" *Bicycling,* January 19, 2018. https://www.bicycling.com/news/a20044419/what-are-sharrows-used-for/

69. Cleveland, Ohio, Municipal Code, Part Four-Traffic Code, Title Five-Vehicles, Chapter 431-Operation Generally, § 431.08(b) (2019), available at https://www.amlegal.com/codes/client/cleveland_oh/

70. Cleveland, Ohio, Municipal Code, Part Four-Traffic Code, Title Seven-Parking, Chapter 451-Parking Generally, § 451.03(a) (17) (2017), available at https://www.amlegal.com/codes/client/cleveland_oh/

71. Cleveland, Ohio, Municipal Code Part Six- Offenses and Business Activities Code, Title l: General Offenses, Chapter 605: Disorderly Conduct and Activity, § 605.10(a)(b)(1) (2008), available at https://www.amlegal.com/codes/client/cleveland_oh/

72. NASCAR, Home page. Accessed September 23, 2019. https://www.nascar.com/

73. de Vroet, Matthew. "How much benefit do we really get from drafting?" Cycling Tips, October 3, 2017. https://cyclingtips.com/2017/10/much-benefit-really-get-drafting/

74. Le Tour de France, Home page. Accessed August 28, 2019. https://www.letour.fr/en/

75. Cleveland Metroparks, Home page. Accessed August 28, 2019. https://www.clevelandmetroparks.com/

76. Bialick, Aaron. "Wiggle Riders to Show Folly of Stop Sign Law by Complying With It." Streetsblog SF, July 27, 2015. https://sf.streetsblog.org/2015/07/27/wiggle-riders-to-show-folly-of-stop-sign-law-by-complying-with-it/

77. 45 Ohio Rev. Code. § 4511.31(B)(3) (2018), available at http://codes.ohio.gov/orc/4511.31

78. Schmitt, Angie. "Arkansas Passes the 'Idaho Stop,' Allowing Cyclists to Treat Red Lights Like Stop Signs." Streetsblog USA, April 3, 2019. https://usa.streetsblog.org/2019/04/03/the-idaho-stop-is-finally-starting-to-happen/

79. Schmitt, Angie. "Oregon Legislature Passes 'Idaho Stop' Bill." Streetsblog USA, June 27, 2019. https://usa.streetsblog.org/2019/06/27/idaho-stop-passes-in-oregon/

80. Washington State Legislature, Bill Information SB 6208 page. Accessed April 2, 2020. https://app.leg.wa.gov/billsummary?BillNumber=6208&Year=2019&Initiative=false

81. "100 Distracted Driving Facts & Statistics for 2018," TeenSafe, December 26, 2018, https://teensafe.com/100-distracted-driving-facts-statistics-for-2018/

82. "2019-2020 NTSB Most Wanted List of Transportation Safety Improvements." National Transportation Board (NTSB). Accessed February 4, 2020. https://www.ntsb.gov/safety/mwl/Documents/2019-20/2019-20-MWL1-Distraction-H.pdf

83. "Ohio Distracted Driving Task Force Report FINAL," Govdelivery. Accessed August 28, 2019. https://content.govdelivery.com/attachments/OHOOD/2019/04/24/file attachments/1198896/Ohio%20Distracted%20Driving%20Task%20Force%20Report%20FINAL.pdf

84. 45 Ohio Rev. Code § 4511.204(A)(B)(1)-(10) (2018), available at http://codes.ohio.gov/orc/4511.204

85. 45 Ohio Rev. Code § 4511.205(A) (2018), available at http://codes.ohio.gov/orc/4511.205

86. The Ohio Legislature. House Bill 95 page. Accessed July 7, 2020. https://www.legislature.ohio.gov/legislation/legislation-status?id=GA132-HB-95

87. "Lakewood City Council Strengthens City's Distracted Driving Laws," City of Lakewood, Ohio; September 26, 2019, http://www.onelakewood.com/lakewood-city-council-strengthens-citys-distracted-driving-laws/

88. "Drunk Driving vs. Distracted Driving: Which is More Dangerous?," The Zebra, June 9, 2017, https://www.thezebra.com/insurance-news/4671/drunk-driving-vs-distracted-driving-dangerous/

89. Ohio Bicycle Federation, Bills We Support page. Accessed August 28, 2019. http://www.ohiobike.org/index.php/advocacy/bills-we-support

90. "New Distracted Driving Council Announced," Mike DeWine, Governor of Ohio, April 25, 2019, https://governor.ohio.gov/wps/portal/gov/governor/media/news-and-media/042519

91. Blundo, Joe. "Widow pushes bill to restrict texting," The Columbus Dispatch, updated September 22, 2011, https://www.dispatch.com/article/20110922/LIFESTYLE/309229713

92. "Rep. Lightbody Introduces Bill To Curb Distracted Driving," The Ohio House of Representatives, Mary Lightbody Press page, January 14, 2020, http://www.ohiohouse.gov/mary-lightbody/press/rep-lightbody-introduces-bill-to-curb-distracted-driving

93. "Distracted Driving," NCSL National Conference of State Legislatures, Research page, October 9, 2019, https://www.ncsl.org/research/transportation/spotlight-distracted-driving.aspx

94. Governor of Ohio Mike DeWine. "Governor DeWine Announces Hands-Free Ohio Bill." February 13, 2020. https://governor.ohio.gov/wps/portal/gov/governor/media/news-and-media/governor-dewine-announces-hands-free-ohio-bill

95. 45 Ohio Rev. Code § 4511.70(C) (2004), available at http://codes.ohio.gov/orc/4511.70

96. Robert Baden-Powell. *Scouting for Boys*, London E.C.: Horace Cox 1908

97. GoPro, Inc., Cameras page. Accessed August 29, 2019. https://shop.gopro.com/cameras

98. Knabe Law Firm Co. L.P.A., Home page. Accessed August 29, 2019. http://klfohio.com/

99. Brouhard, Rod. "An Overview of Traumatic Brain Injury." *VeryWellHealth*, updated September 17, 2019. https://www.verywellhealth.com/difference-between-concussions-and-traumatic-brain-injuries-4126107

100. Rosenthal, Michele. "The Science Behind PTSD Symptoms: How Trauma Changes The Brain." *PsychCentral*, updated June 27, 2019. https://psychcentral.com/blog/the-science-behind-ptsd-symptoms-how-trauma-changes-the-brain/

101. Ohio City Incorporated, Home page. Accessed September 27, 2019. http://www.ohiocity.org/

102. With permission of Ashley Shaw.

103. Velosurance, Why bicycle insurance? page. Accessed August 29, 2019. https://velosurance.com

104. Regional Cite: State v. Patrick, 914 N.E.2d 1121 (Mun. Ct. 2008)

105. State v. Gatto, 2007-Ohio-4609 (Ct. App.) (6th district)

106. Regional - *State v. Tudor*, 118 N.E.3d 297 (Ohio Ct. App. 2019); Public domain - *State v. Tudor*, 2019-Ohio-24 (11th Dist. Ct. App.)

107. State v. Copley, 8th Dist. Cuyahoga No. 92784, 2010-Ohio-2340 (May 27, 2010)

108. Full Regional Cite: Cummings v. Lyles, 27 N.E.3d 985 (Ohio, Ct. App. 2015)

109. Passwaters v. Knaur, 2006-Ohio-1518 (Ct. App.)

110. Full Regional Cite: Deutsch v. Birk, 937 N.E.2d 638 (Ohio, Ct. App. 2010); Full Official Reporter Cite: Deutsch v. Birk, 189 Ohio App. 3d 129 (2010); Short Cite: Deutsch, 937 N.E.2d at 638

111. Crabtree v. Cook, 964 N.E.2d 473 (Ohio Ct. App. 2011)

112. Ohio Unreported Format: Storc v. Day Drive Assocs. Ltd., 8th Dist. Cuyahoga No. 86284, 2006-Ohio-561 (Feb. 9, 2006)

113. Kane v. City of Dayton, Montgomery Cty. C.P. Ct. No. 2017-CV-04722 (2018)

114. "2019 Bike Friendly State Report Cards." The League of American Bicyclists. Accessed January 7, 2020. https://bikeleague.org/content/state-report-cards

115. "New Report Ranks Cleveland Drivers Among Worst in the Country." Tittle Law Firm. Accessed February 4, 2020. https://tittlelawfirm.com/new-report-ranks-cleveland-drivers-among-worst-in-the-country/

116. Bike Cleveland, Vision Zero page. Accessed May 4, 2020. https://www.bikecleveland.org/visionzero/

117. "2018 Fatal Motor Vehicle Crashes: Overview." National Highway Traffic Safety Administration (NHTSA), October 2019. https://crashstats.nhtsa.dot.gov/Api/Public/ViewPublication/812826

118. "U.S. Transportation Secretary Elaine L. Chao Announces Further Decreases in Roadway Fatalities", National Highway Traffic Safety Administration, October 22, 2019, https://www.nhtsa.gov/press-releases/roadway-fatalities-2018-fars

119. Spin Bike Shop, Home page. Accessed October 2, 2019. http://www.spinbikeshop.com

120. Gear Up Velo, Home page. Accessed April 1, 2020. https://www.gearupvelo.com/

121. "State Electric Bicycle Laws | A Legislative Primer," National Conference of State Legislatures, March 28, 2019, https://www.ncsl.org/research/transportation/state-electric-bicycle-laws-a-legislative-primer.aspx

122. Ibid.

123. The Ohio Legislature, House Bill 250 page. Accessed July 7, 2020. https://www.legislature.ohio.gov/legislation/legislation-status?id=GA132-HB-250

124. "State Electric Bicycle Laws | A Legislative Primer," National Conference of State Legislatures, March 28, 2019, https://www.ncsl.org/research/transportation/state-electric-bicycle-laws-a-legislative-primer.aspx

125. 45 Ohio Rev. Code § 4511.01(SSS) (2019), available at http://codes.ohio.gov/orc/4511.01

126. 45 Ohio Rev. Code § 4511.01(TTT) (2019), available at http://codes.ohio.gov/orc/4511.01

127. 45 Ohio Rev. Code § 4511.01(UUU) (2019), available at http://codes.ohio.gov/orc/4511.01

128. 45 Ohio Rev. Code § 4511.522 (D)(2)(2019), available at http://codes.ohio.gov/orc/4511.522

129. 45 Ohio Rev. Code § 4511.522 (D)(1)(2019), available at http://codes.ohio.gov/orc/4511.522

130. "Can I Ride My E-Bike There?" Bike Cleveland. Accessed March 11, 2020. https://www.bikecleveland.org/bike-cle/news/e-bike/2018/12/?fbclid=IwAR0D GVD3l7RKXQaSQ1nxyadJjlKXiwT96vGqN f8JvTIUyM18lzyQrkHLg

131. 45 Ohio Rev. Code § 4511.522(C)(1) (2019), available at http://codes.ohio.gov/orc/4511.522

132. 45 Ohio Rev. Code § 4511.522(C)(2) (2019), available at http://codes.ohio.gov/orc/4511.522

133. 45 Ohio Rev. Code § 4511.522(C)(3) (2019), available at http://codes.ohio.gov/orc/4511.522

134. McFarland, Matt. "Lyft launches a scooter service. Uber is close behind." CNN Business, September 6, 2018. https://money.cnn.com/2018/09/06/technology/lyft-scooters-denver-uber/index.html

135. The Ohio Legislature, House Bill 295 page. Accessed November 12, 2019. https://www.legislature.ohio.gov/legislation/legislation-status?id=GA133-HB-295

136. Higgs, Robert. "Cleveland to allow electric scooter rentals this summer, targeting key parts of the city for pilot program." *Plain Dealer* (Cleveland, Ohio), updated December 6, 2019. https://www.cleveland.com/cityhall/2019/06/cleveland-to-

allow-electric-scooter-rentals-this-summer-targeting-key-in-parts-of-the-city-for-pilot-program.html

137. Bamforth, Emily. "Bird electric scooters spotted in Cleveland." *Plain Dealer* (Cleveland, Ohio), updated January 30, 2019. https://www.cleveland.com/metro/2018/08/bird_electric_scooters_spotted.html

138. Cleveland, Ohio, Municipal Code Part Four-Traffic Code, Title IX: Pedestrians, Bicycles and Motorcycles, Chapter 473: Bicycles, Motorcycles and Mobility Devices, § 473.02(b)(6) (2019), available at https://www.amlegal.com/codes/client/cleveland_oh/

139. Cleveland, Ohio, Municipal Code Part Four-Traffic Code, Title IX: Pedestrians, Bicycles and Motorcycles, Chapter 473: Bicycles, Motorcycles and Mobility Devices, § 473.02(b)(5) (2019), available at https://www.amlegal.com/codes/client/cleveland_oh/

140. Cleveland, Ohio, Municipal Code Part Four-Traffic Code, Title IX: Pedestrians, Bicycles and Motorcycles, Chapter 473: Bicycles, Motorcycles and Mobility Devices, § 473.10(a)(b)(c) (2019), available at https://www.amlegal.com/codes/client/cleveland_oh/

141. Cleveland, Ohio, Municipal Code Part Four-Traffic Code, Title IX: Pedestrians, Bicycles and Motorcycles, Chapter 473: Bicycles, Motorcycles and Mobility Devices, § 473.10(d) (2019), available at https://www.amlegal.com/codes/client/cleveland_oh/

142. "City of Cleveland Issues Shared Mobility Permit to Wheels." City of Cleveland. September 24, 2019. http://city.cleveland.oh.us/09.24.2019SharedMobilityWheels

143. Cleveland, Ohio, Municipal Code Part Four- Traffic Code, Title I: Administration, Chapter 401: Definitions, § 401.231 (2019), available at https://www.amlegal.com/codes/client/cleveland_oh/

144. Wheels Support Center, Can I ride in the rain? page, accessed March 11, 2020. https://getwheelsapp.zendesk.com/hc/en-us/articles/360022741672-Can-I-ride-in-the-rain-

145. Wikipedia, Self-driving car page. Accessed July 7, 2020. https://en.wikipedia.org/wiki/Self-driving_car#Incidents

146. Jochem, Todd. "They Drove Cross-Country in an Autonomous Minivan Without GPS. In 1995." Jalopnik, April 9, 2015. https://jalopnik.com/they-drove-cross-country-in-an-autonomous-minivan-witho-1696330141

147. Wikipedia, Self-driving car page. Accessed July 7, 2020. https://en.wikipedia.org/wiki/Self-driving_car#Incidents

148. Teale, Chris. "Federal AV legislation to go no further in Congress." Smart Cities Dive, December 21, 2018. https://www.smartcitiesdive.com/news/AV-START-Act-autonomous-vehicle-legislation/544907/

149. "Autonomous Vehicles | Self-Driving Vehicles Enacted Legislation", National Conference of State Legislatures (NCSL), February 18, 2020. https://www.ncsl.org/research/transportation/autonomous-vehicles-self-driving-vehicles-enacted-legislation.aspx

150. Wikipedia, DriveOhio page. Accessed July 7, 2020. https://en.wikipedia.org/wiki/DriveOhio

151. Bischoff, Laura A. "Driverless vehicles being tested at 4,500-acre Ohio site." *Dayton Daily News*, November 26, 2019. https://www.daytondailynews.com/news/local/driverless-vehicles-being-tested-500-acre-ohio-site/GCBRBChr1LIS65dD6LzZ7I/

152. The League of American Bicyclists, Automated Vehicles page. Accessed August 29, 2019. https://www.bikeleague.org/content/automated-vehicles

153. "NHTSA Announces Coming Upgrades to New Car Assessment Program." National Highway Traffic Safety

Administration (NHTSA). October 16, 2019. https://www.nhtsa.gov/press-releases/ncap-upgrades-coming

154. National Highway Traffic Safety Administration. Dummy Management page. Accessed July 13, 2020. https://one.nhtsa.gov/Research/Dummy-Management

155. Edmonds, Ellen. "AAA Warns Pedestrian Detection Systems Don't Work When Needed Most." AAA, October 3, 2019. https://newsroom.aaa.com/2019/10/aaa-warns-pedestrian-detection-systems-dont-work-when-needed-most/

156. U.S. Department of Transportation, Fact Sheet: Fixing America's Surface Transportation Act or "FAST Act" page, accessed July 13, 2020. https://www.fhwa.dot.gov/fastact/factsheets/transportationalternativesfs.cfm

157. Vuocolo, Alex. "Bike to Work? This Bill in Congress Would Give You a Tax Deduction." *Bicycling*, March 14, 2019. https://www.bicycling.com/news/a26822870/bicycle-commuter-act/

158. Library of Congress, H.R. 1507 page. Accessed July 13, 2020. https://www.congress.gov/bill/116th-congress/house-bill/1507/all-info

159. Library of Congress, S.2302 page. Accessed July 13,2020. https://www.congress.gov/bill/116th-congress/senate-bill/2302/actions?q=%7B%22search%22%3A%5B%22S+2302%22%5D%7D&r=1&s=1

160. "Senate Committee Transportation Bill is a Win for Bike Funding," PeopleForBikes, July 31, 2019, https://peopleforbikes.org/blog/senate-committee-transportation-bill-is-a-win-for-bike-funding/

161. The Ohio Legislature. House Bill 97 page. Accessed July 7, 2020. https://www.legislature.ohio.gov/legislation/legislation-summary?id=GA133-HB-97

162. Durant, Maria. "New bill pushing statewide ban on distracted driving, making it a primary offense," *ABC6*, accessed July 13, 2020, https://abc6onyourside.com/news/local/new-bill-

pushing-statewide-ban-on-distracted-driving-making-it-a-primary-offense

163. The Ohio Legislature. House Bill 468 page. Accessed July 7, 2020. https://www.legislature.ohio.gov/legislation/legislation-summary?id=GA133-HB-468

164. The Ohio Legislature. House Bill 710 page. Accessed July 7, 2020. https://www.legislature.ohio.gov/legislation/legislation-summary?id=GA133-HB-710

165. The Ohio Legislature. Senate Bill 73 page. Accessed July 7, 2020. https://www.legislature.ohio.gov/legislation/legislation-summary?id=GA133-SB-73

166. Cleveland Metropolitan School District, Safe Routes to School page. Accessed July 13, 2020. https://www.clevelandmetroschools.org/saferoutes

167. Ohio Department of Transportation, Fact Sheet: Walk.Bike.Ohio page, accessed July 13, 2020. http://www.dot.state.oh.us/WalkBike/Documents/ODOT_FactSheet_v4.pdf

168. Kilpatrick, Mary. "Cuyahoga Greenways imagines network of bike paths, trails, bike friendly streets across the county." *Plain Dealer* (Cleveland, Ohio), updated April 29, 2019. https://www.cleveland.com/metro/2019/04/cuyahoga-greenways-imagines-network-of-bike-paths-trails-bike-friendly-streets-across-the-county.html

169. Wikipedia, Complete streets page. Accessed July 13, 2020. https://en.wikipedia.org/wiki/Complete_streets

170. Litt, Steven. "NOACA boosts protected bike lane projects in Cleveland with spending package." *Plain Dealer* (Cleveland, OH), updated January 11, 2019. https://www.cleveland.com/architecture/2017/12/noaca_boosts_protected_bike_la.html

171. Bike Cleveland, Midway Protected Bike Network page. Accessed October 3, 2019. https://www.bikecleveland.org/midway/

172. Bike Cleveland, Vision Zero page. Accessed May 4, 2020. https://www.bikecleveland.org/visionzero/

173. Leizerman & Young, Home page. Accessed July 13, 2020. https://www.truckaccidents.com/

174. Knabe Law Firm, Vision Zero page. Accessed July 15, 2020. https://klfohio.com/wp-content/uploads/2020/07/Vision-Zero-Subcommittee-Contact-List.pdf

175. U.S. Department of Transportation/Federal Highway Administration, National Bicycling and Walking Study. Accessed July 13, 2020. https://safety.fhwa.dot.gov/ped_bike/docs/case15.pdf

176. Davis, Jonita. "The Pros for the Environment of Riding Bikes." SFGate. Accessed July 13, 2020. https://homeguides.sfgate.com/pros-environment-riding-bikes-79378.html

177. Friedman, Michael S., et al. "Impact of Changes in Transportation and Commuting Behaviors During the 1996 Summer Olympic Games in Atlanta on Air Quality and Childhood Asthma," abstract, *American Journal of Preventive Medicine (AJPM)* 285, no. 7 (February 2001): 897-905, doi:10.1001/jama.285.7.897.

178. Green, Josh. "Bike Lanes & Property Values: Is There A Correlation?" CURBED Atlanta, August 8, 2013. https://atlanta.curbed.com/2013/8/8/10210634/bike-lanes-property-values-is-there-a-correlation

179. Lown-Hecht, Tania. "The Nantahala and Pisgah National Forests: An Economic Powerhouse for Western North Carolina." Outdoor Alliance, October 4, 2017. https://www.outdooralliance.org/blog/2017/10/4/the-nantahala-and-pisgah-national-forests-an-economic-powerhouse-for-western-north-carolina-1

180. Walton Family Foundation. "Bicycling Provides $137 Million in Economic Benefits to Northwest Arkansas." News release, March 29, 2018. Walton Family Foundation. Accessed July

24, 2020. https://www.waltonfamilyfoundation.org/about-us/newsroom/bicycling-provides-137-million-in-economic-benefits-to-northwest-arkansas

181. Gutierrez-Jones, Jackie. "All the Right Moves." Livability, accessed July 13, 2020. https://livability.com/sites/default/files/2018-10/Livability%20Trend%20Report%20Millennials.pdf

182. Murnane, Kevin. "New Research Indicates Cycling To Work Has Extraordinary Health Benefits." Forbes, April 25, 2017. https://www.forbes.com/sites/kevinmurnane/2017/04/25/new-research-indicates-cycling-to-work-has-extraordinary-health-benefits/#7c7919443e62

183. Sugiyama, Takemi. "Commuting by Car: Weight Gain Among Physically Active Adults," abstract, *American Journal of Preventive Medicine (AJPM) 44*, no. 2 (February 2013): 169-173, doi: 10.1016/j.amepre.2012.09.063. https://www.ajpmonline.org/article/S0749-3797(12)00776-3/abstract

WA